EMOTION AND REASON IN CONSUMER BEHAVIOR

EMOTION AND REASON IN CONSUMER BEHAVIOR

Arjun Chaudhuri

Fairfield University

ELSEVIER

AMSTERDAM • BOSTON • HEIDELBERG • LONDON
NEW YORK • OXFORD • PARIS • SAN DIEGO
SAN FRANCISCO • SINGAPORE • SYDNEY • TOKYO

Butterworth-Heinemann is an imprint of Elsevier

Butterworth-Heinemann is an imprint of Elsevier
30 Corporate Drive, Suite 400, Burlington, MA 01803, USA
Linacre House, Jordan Hill, Oxford OX2 8DP, UK

∞ Recognizing the importance of preserving what has been written, Elsevier prints its
books on acid-free paper whenever possible.

Library of Congress Cataloging-in-Publication Data
Chaudhuri, Arjun.
    Emotion and reason in consumer behavior / Arjun Chaudhuri.
        p.   cm.
    Includes bibliographical references and index.
    ISBN-13: 978-0-7506-7976-3   ISBN-10: 0-7506-7976-X (alk. paper)
    1. Consumer behavior.   2. Consumer behavior—Psychological aspects.   I. Title.

    HF5415.32.C45 2005
    658.8'342—dc22

                                                                        2005052084

British Library Cataloguing-in-Publication Data
A catalogue record for this book is available from the British Library.

ISBN-13: 978-0-7506-7976-3
ISBN-10: 0-7506-7976-X

For information on all Academic Press publications
visit our Web site at www.books.elsevier.com

Printed in the United States of America
06 07 08 09 10   10 9 8 7 6 5 4 3 2

This book is for
my wife, Kathleen,
and my mother, Nilima.

CONTENTS

FOREWORD

Ross Buck

Department of Communication
Sciences and Psychology
University of Connecticut, Storrs

Emotion and Reason in Consumer Behavior is a pioneering book, among the first if not the first to apply systematic emotion theory and measurement techniques to the analysis of consumer behavior. I am confident that it will not be the last. Emotion was long a difficult notion in the social and behavioral sciences because of the perceived difficulty of measuring one of its core components: subjective experience. Behaviorists almost entirely eschewed the concept of emotion because it appeared to be impossible to objectively measure and verify subjective experiences because they appear essentially to be "private events." B. F. Skinner (1953) acknowledged that private events "may be distinguished by limited accessibility but not, so far as we know, by any special structure or nature" (p. 257). Presciently, Skinner also noted, "the line between public and private is not fixed. The boundary shifts with every discovery of a technique for making private events public. . . . The problem of privacy may, therefore, eventually be solved by technical advances" (p. 282). With the coming of the cognitive revolution, emotions came to be seen as disturbances that occur when cognitive processing is disrupted (Miller, Galanter, & Pribram, 1960; Simon, 1967). However, subjective experience per se was seen as private and unobservable, and self-report measures of emotional experience were suspect because they could not be objectively confirmed.

When the study of emotion began to gain scientific respectability beginning in the late 1960s, it was its objectively observable display and communicative aspects rather than its experiential aspects that were emphasized. An important sign of this rebirth was the work of Paul Ekman, E. R. Sorenson, and Wallace Friesen, published in *Science* (1969), which demonstrated that the posed facial expressions of Westerners can accurately be interpreted by isolated Fore tribespeople in highland New Guinea, and that the Fore's expressions could be interpreted by Americans. Similarly, the work of Robert E. Miller showed that normal rhesus monkeys can demonstrate accurate spontaneous emotional communication, which can, however, be disrupted by such factors as early isolation and certain psychoactive drugs (Miller, Caul, & Mirsky, 1967).

The Developmental-Interactionist theory of emotion stemmed from my work with Miller, applying his techniques for measuring spontaneous emotional communication to human beings (Buck, 1976, 1984). The theory viewed affect and reason as interacting in a developmental context. It saw emotion as an aspect of a "filter" that responds quickly to events prior to complex information processing, and indeed emotion was seen to alter and guide higher-order processing. This kind of conceptualization received important support in the work of Joseph LeDoux (1996), who demonstrated that the brain responds to affective events in two ways: with a fast but relatively undifferentiated "low road" system involving emotion mechanisms in the subcortical and old-cortical parts of the brain, and with a slower but more differentiated "high road" involving new-cortical mechanisms. The "low road" information functions to quickly command attention and physiological arousal, and to stimulate reflexive action; the "high road" modulates the low road reaction and initiates goal-oriented coping behaviors. So, when you are startled by your playful roommate, the initial "low road" emotional response is quickly followed by relief that it is just your roommate playing a trick.

Recent studies have used technical advances that actually do give a measure of accessibility to otherwise "private events" as Skinner (1953) had suggested. This includes functional magnetic resonance imaging—the fMRI—that by mapping blood flow determines which parts of the brain are activated. For example, Arthur Aron, Helen Fisher, Lucy Brown, and colleagues (2005) recently showed that pictures of a loved one shown to persons in a state of acute romantic love activate subcortical reward areas including the right ventral tegmental area and dorsal caudate. Importantly, Aron stated in a June 2005 press release that the strong relationships demonstrated in this research between self-reported romantic love and specific brain activity "dramatically increase our confidence that self-report questionnaires can actually measure brain activity." Another recent study illustrates that basic neurochemicals can induce complex behavior patterns in human beings. Kosfeld et al. (2005) showed that the simple administration of the neurohormone oxytocin—linked to nurturance in animals—increases the trust that people have in strangers.

This analysis and research illustrate two routes to cognition (or knowledge)—one affective and the other rational—and it also suggests that emotion can be a cause as well as an effect of information processing. The importance of the affective side in decision making was affirmed in the work of Daniel Kahneman (2003), who distinguished "effortless intuition" from "deliberative rationality," and demonstrated in contrast with many cognitive theorists that intuition can often promote and enhance effective decision making. This has important implications for understanding information processing and decision making and their application to consumer behavior. It is clear that emotional appeals are often powerful and effective in advertising and marketing; this work suggests reasons why that is so, and opens up a whole new world of testable hypotheses.

Don Tucker (1981) coined the term *syncretic cognition* to apply to affective cognition: It is direct and holistic, synthesizing information. In contrast, *analytic cognition* is linear and sequential. Arjun Chaudhuri and I used Tucker's terms to apply to rational and affective cognition, which was the basis of the Communication via Analytic and Syncretic Cognition (CASC) scale (Buck, Anderson, Chaudhuri, & Ray, 2004; Buck & Chaudhuri, 1994; Buck, Chaudhuri, Georgson, & Kowta, 1995). One of the assumptions behind this scale was that measuring emotional experience by self-reports is not only possible, but also rather straightforward; indeed it is potentially easier than many reports reflecting rational processing. The CASC scale is also a flexible instrument, able to assess many emotions that have been passed over by traditional emotion theories. For example, in addition to the individualistic "primary affects" of Ekman and colleagues—happiness, sadness, fear, anger, surprise, and disgust—the CASC scale can assess "reptilian" emotions involving sex and power; "prosocial" emotions of love, nurturance, bonding, and attachment; "social" emotions of pride/arrogance, guilt/shame, envy/jealousy, and pity/scorn; and "moral" emotions including admiration, resentment, humiliation, sympathy, trust, respect, and hope (Buck, 1999, 2002, 2004).

Arjun Chaudhuri validated the CASC scale (Chaudhuri & Buck, 1995, 1998) and applied it in analyzing responses to consumer products in an outstanding program of careful and systematic empirical research. The success of this effort is demonstrated convincingly in *Emotion and Reason in Consumer Behavior*. In addition, this book provides many other important insights into the role of the dynamic emotion–reason relationship in consumer behavior. It blazes a new trail in the analysis of consumer behavior: one that will be followed by many.

Ross W. Buck
Storrs, Connecticut
June 2005

REFERENCES

Aron, A., Fisher, H. E., Mashek, D. J., Strong, G., Li, H-F., and Brown, L. L. (2005). Reward, motivation and emotion systems associated with early-stage intense romantic love. *Journal of Neurophysiology, 93*(6). In press.

Buck, R. (1976). *Human motivation and emotion.* New York: John Wiley & Sons. (2nd ed., 1988; Japanese ed., 2002).

Buck, R. (1984). *The communication of emotion.* New York: Guilford Press.

Buck, R. (1999). The biological affects: A typology. *Psychological Review, 106,* 301–336.

Buck, R. (2002). The genetics and biology of true love: Prosocial biological affects and the left hemisphere. *Psychological Review, 109,* 739–744.

Buck, R. (2004). The gratitude of exchange and the gratitude of caring: A developmental-interactionist perspective of moral emotion. In R. A. Emmons & M. McCullough (Eds.), *The psychology of gratitude* (pp. 100–122). New York: Oxford University Press.

Buck, R., Anderson, E., Chaudhuri, A., and Ray, I. (2004). Emotion and reason in persuasion: Applying the ARI Model and the CASC Scale. *Journal of Business Research. Marketing Communications and Consumer Behavior, 57*(6), 647–656.

Buck, R., & Chaudhuri, A. (1994). Affect, reason, and involvement in persuasion: The ARI Model. In Forschungsgruppe Konsum und Verhalten (Hrsg.). *Konsumenten forschung* [*Consumer research*] (pp. 107–117). Munchen: Verlag Franz Vahlen.

Buck, R., Chaudhuri, A., Georgson, M., & Kowta, S. (1995). Conceptualizing and operationalizing affect, reason, and involvement in persuasion: The ARI Model and the CASC Scale. In F. Kardes & M. Sujan (Eds.), *Advances in consumer research.* (Vol. 22, pp. 1–8). Provo, UT: Association for Consumer Research.

Chaudhuri, A., & Buck, R. (1995). An exploration of triune brain effects in advertising. In F. Kardes & M. Sujan (Eds.), *Advances in consumer research* (Vol. 22, pp. 133–138). Provo, UT: Association for Consumer Research.

Chaudhuri, A., & Buck, R. (1998). CASC—Eine Skala zur Messung Emotionaler und Rationaler Reaktionen auf Werbebotschaften. *Zeitschrift fuer Sozialpsychologie, 29*(2), 194–206.

Ekman, P., Sorenson, E. R., & Friesen, W. V. (1969). Pan-cultural elements in facial displays of emotions. *Science, 164*(3875), 86–88.

Kahneman, D. (2003). A perspective on judgment and choice: Mapping bounded rationality. *American Psychologist, 58,* 697–720.

Kosfeld, M., Heinrichs, M., Zak, P. J., Fischbacher, U., & Fehr, E. (2005). Oxytocin increases trust in humans. *Nature, 435,* 673–676.

LeDoux, J. (1996). *The emotional brain.* New York: Simon & Schuster.

Miller, G. A., Galanter, E., & Pribram, K. H. (1960). *Plans and the structure of behavior.* New York: Henry Holt.

Miller, R. E., Caul, W. F., & Mirsky, I. A. (1967). Communication of affects between feral and socially isolated monkeys. *Journal of Personality and Social Psychology, 7,* 231–239.

Simon, H. A. (1967). Motivational and emotional controls of cognition. *Psychological Review, 74,* 29–39.

Skinner, B. F. (1953). *Science and human behavior.* New York: Macmillan.

Tucker, D. (1981). Lateral brain function, emotion, and conceptualization. *Psychological Bulletin, 89,* 19–46.

AUTHOR'S NOTE

Emotions, passions, sentiments, and feelings have pervaded my life. One of my earliest memories hangs like an ornate Dutch painting in my mind. It is night and our servant, Ramesh, is crouching on the marble floor of our old Calcutta house, picking up the pieces of a broken vase. His frightened eyes dart to where my father stands. My father hovers over him like some dark and dreadful avenger, his rage flowing through every muscle in his taut body. The only chandelier in the room sparkles on the huge silver buckle on my father's belt. At the other end of the long, heavily draped living room, a 4-year-old boy, stricken with conscience and fear, hides his face in his mother's lap. She looks at him with the compassion of an angel who must stand by and allow mere mortals to choose their own destiny.

I chose well that night and was rewarded by flashy grins and extra helpings from Ramesh as he served dinner. My mother called me her "little man," and over the comfort of dinner I remember feeling quite heroic in my earlier tearful admission of guilt—"I broke the vase, Daddy." My father stayed in his room, having eaten earlier, displeased over the fuss. Even my two older sisters, who usually considered me to be a demon incarnate, looked happily in my direction. All this I remember vividly although it happened so long ago. Mundane things fade from the mind but emotions from the past linger on as reminders of who we were, where we have been, and what we are.

This book is about how emotion affects consumer behavior. In the last 25 years or so, the role of emotion in information processing has been widely acknowledged, and scholars have shown that we need to understand both emotion and reason if we want to understand the real meanings that products and services have for consumers. This has had immense ramifications for advertising, marketing, and other domains of persuasive intercourse in today's "brave new world." As our world comes closer together, "global" messages, which transcend cultural boundaries, become more appropriate than localized messages for particular cultures. Emotion is a language that is understood by all people regardless of their local habitats. With a swish, Nike speaks to the whole world. With a few cute polar bears, Coke befriends consumers from Bermuda to Bangkok. With a smile on CNN, a politician appears warm and kind to the electronic global village. Emotion via nonverbal communication is the language of humanity and it brings us closer together.

The purpose of this book, then, is to understand and describe some of the emotional and rational reasons for consumers' choices of products and their processing of commercial messages. I also hope to be able to show some of the effects these motivational forces have on marketing outcomes such as brand loyalty, market share, higher price margins, and so forth. I have written this book for both graduate and undergraduate students. All the chapters have a theoretical section and a "research results" section at the end of the chapter. The latter section will probably appeal more to graduate students, but I hope that whoever reads this text will also take some time to see the evidence that is sometimes cited in support of the theoretical ideas in the text. Sometimes the research results are only intended to amplify selected aspects of the text. In other chapters, the research results are intended to show the evidence, if any, for the entire model in the chapter. Hopefully, some of what I have learned and absorbed about emotion and reason will stimulate the reader to pursue further explorations in this vast and mysterious field.

This book is based on some of the research that I have conducted, over the last 20 years or so, on the role of emotion and reason in various consumer behavior phenomena. It is certainly not intended to be a consumer behavior book in the normal sense. It is more a compilation of some of my own investigations and experiences on various, sometimes disparate, topics than a comprehensive summary of the consumer behavior field. Nor do I mean to suggest that other work on emotion in consumer behavior does not exist. My own work pales in comparison to the massive literature on the topic, which already exists, and to which so may people have so handsomely contributed. At the same time, because all consumer behavior phenomena are rooted in the human mind, I believe that this book, no matter how incomplete, serves to highlight the importance of emotion and reason as the basic, primal, and quintessential elements of the human mind and, indeed, of all consumer behavior in general. Perhaps, one day, there will be a comprehensive text on emotion and reason in consumer behavior (and I will tip my hat to whoever undertakes such a magnificent task!), but that was not my intention with this modest offering. Perhaps this small beginning will encourage someone else to undertake a larger adventure on the subject.

I am extremely grateful to Fairfield University for giving me a place in academia from which to conduct my explorations in emotion and reason. The administrative and academic community at this extraordinary Jesuit institution has always encouraged my scholarship. I owe much to my past and present deans and to my colleagues in the Charles F. Dolan School of Business at Fairfield University. I must also thank all those who have helped me directly in my work over the last two decades. This includes my students, all my professors in graduate school, editors and reviewers of journals, colleagues at conferences, co-authors of papers, and people in the advertising and marketing professions. Thanks to Michael Basta for patiently helping me with the preparation of the manuscript. Thanks also to Jane MacDonald at Elsevier for her gracious encouragement of this project.

I must specially thank my two mentors at the University of Connecticut, Ross Buck and Jim Watt, who taught me how to think about emotion. With their help, I have tried to understand emotion and, in doing so, I have been able to calm my own fears and raise my glass to the simple things in life.

Arjun Chaudhuri
Fairfield University,
Fairfield, Connecticut
June 2005

I

INTRODUCTION

"When you understand all about the sun and all about the atmosphere and all about the rotation of the Earth, you may still miss the radiance of the sunset."

(Jane Fonda, quoting Alfred North Whitehead at
the graduation ceremony in 1994 of Emma
Willard School, Troy, NY)

Consumer behavior is the study of how and why people consume products and services. All behavior can broadly be attributed to three classic influences—the particular characteristics of the individual, the environment that surrounds the individual, and the inherited genetics that constitute the biological makeup of the individual.

The characteristics of the individual consist of, among others, the personality, perceptions, attitudes, needs, and motivations of the individual. The environment of the individual consists of the culture, subculture, family, friends, and institutions that the individual lives in. The genetics of an individual are the biological codes that are unique to each individual, such as DNA, and which are passed on to the progeny of the individual.

The model in Figure 1.1 shows that stimuli (marketing, etc.) result in emotional and rational responses in the individual's mind, which, in turn, may lead to a particular behavioral response by the individual. The model also shows that the nature of these emotional and rational responses is also affected by a host of influences under the general categories of the individual's personal characteristics, environment, and genetics. Thus, for instance, an advertisement is interpreted according to the culture of the individual and then produces a happy (or unhappy) response in the individual and prompts the individual to buy (or not to buy) the advertised brand.

DEFINING EMOTION AND REASON

Emotions such as joy and sorrow are basic, primal motivations in the human condition, and they are also crucial determinants in our choices of products and services and in our processing of commercial messages like advertising.

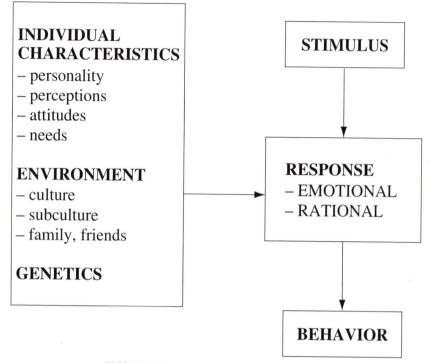

FIGURE I.I   A Model of Consumer Behavior.

In addition, choices of products and services are also based on ratiocination and reason; consumers analyze and process information in terms of the attributes of products and services in order to arrive at an optimal decision concerning their alternative choices. Thus, consumers assign both emotional and rational values to products and services, and the study of these values is critical to the understanding of marketing and consumer behavior. To cite Belk (1988), "We cannot hope to understand consumer behavior without first gaining some understanding of the meanings that consumers attach to possessions" (p. 139).

These "meanings" reside in the archetypal constructs of emotion and reason, which may be viewed as two separate yet often complementary means of gaining knowledge about the world. Emotion and reason may be defined as knowledge by acquaintance and knowledge by description, respectively. "Knowledge by acquaintance" (emotion) is immediate and direct subjective experience that is "known" as self-evident. This is the process which William James (1890) wrote about: "I know the color blue when I see it, and the flavor of a pear when I taste it . . . but about the inner nature of these facts or what makes them what they are I can say nothing at all" (p. 22).

In contrast, "knowledge by description" (reason) results from the interpretation of sensory data and involves judgments about phenomena. As Bertrand Russell (1912) observed, "My knowledge of a table as a physical object . . . is not direct knowledge. Such as it is, it is obtained through acquaintance with the sense-data that make up the appearance of the table" (pp. 73–74). Thus, the brain appears to involve two functionally different ways of knowing. Knowledge by acquaintance (emotion) is the holistic and synthetic integration of sensory data from the external and internal bodily environments. In contrast, knowledge by description (reason) is the sequential and analytic processing of information based on an appraisal of the environment (Buck, 1988; Tucker, 1981).

An example may help here. Think about your response to music. If you are an average music listener you probably do not think of "B flats" and "C minors" when you hear a piece of music. That would be a rational reaction to music or knowledge of music by description (i.e., you could describe the piece to someone else in terms of the musical notations, and if they spoke the same "language," they would be able to understand your meaning). But, if you are like me, you probably just react spontaneously or emotionally to music and you "know" quite well whether you like the piece or not, but you cannot really describe it to someone else. You know the music by acquaintance, or by your own emotional response to it. I have "known" the music of Nat King Cole all my life and loved it, but I could never really properly describe it to you. I might tell you that it was "great" and "beautiful" and "uplifting," but those would just be adjectives. To really feel the music, you would have to hear it for yourself. Emotions cannot really be described. They have to be experienced firsthand.

THE COMMUNICATION OF EMOTION AND REASON

Thus, emotion and reason are both ways of "knowing" and understanding reality, but they work very differently. As described by Buck (1984), emotion can be spontaneously communicated, whereas rational messages are symbolically communicated. Thus, communication of a stimulus has two aspects—spontaneous and symbolic. Spontaneous communication is biologically shared, nonintentional or automatic, and nonpropositional. It requires only knowledge by acquaintance and is expressed through signs that make motivational-emotional states externally accessible. Symbolic communication is socially shared, intentional, and propositional. It requires knowledge by description and is based upon learned symbols, which have a learned and arbitrary relationship with their referents. These are two simultaneous streams of communication that usually interact and modify one another. It must be stressed that these are not two ends on a single continuum, but instead represent two independent yet interactive dimensions. However, although "pure" spontaneous communication is possible, "pure" symbolic communication is not. In other words, symbolic communication is always accompanied by spontaneous communication (Buck, 1984).

As an example, what would be spontaneous and symbolic communication in a television commercial? Anything nonverbal would be spontaneous communication: the facial expressions of the actors (even though these are obviously rehearsed!), the color and settings in the ad, and so on. Anything to do with a language that uses symbols to convey meaning would be symbolic communication. So, the words on a television screen and spoken words would be symbolic as would mathematical notations, if any. We have already seen that music could be both. The audio portion would be spontaneous communication. If any musical notation (as in a score sheet) was in the ad then that would be symbolic.

Symbolic communication can also sometimes lead to emotional outcomes. In fact, Buck (1984) says that symbolic communication is always accompanied by some spontaneous elements. Buck also says that some spontaneous communication is "pure" and without symbolic elements. Words, for instance, can sometimes have nonverbal meanings, say through tone, pitch, or rhythm. These are called "vocalics" in nonverbal communication. Also, words sometimes arouse emotions, as in a novel or poem or speech or advertising copy.

FORMS OF EMOTIONS

There are various forms of emotions and various types within these forms. According to Buck (1985, 1988, 1999), emotion takes the following forms:

- Emotion I (EI), consisting of physiological responses like heart rate changes, blood pressure, sweating, and so on, which are altered in order to support action. This serves to adapt the body to changes in the environment and to keep it in equilibrium.
- Emotion II (EII), which is spontaneous, expressive behavior, such as facial expressions, gestures, posture, and the like, and which serves the function of social coordination. Although display rules may affect this behavior, these responses, by being accessible to others, reveal a person's motivational-emotional state. Further, the responses of others to such spontaneous expression help the person to understand and label their feelings, and a social process is established that controls behavior. With regard to "display rules," note that certain situations can inhibit the display of spontaneous feelings. There are also cultural rules about shows of emotion. These can vary by gender as well. Another example of "less than

truthful" displays occurs when people practice deceit in their expressions.

- Emotion III (EIII), is immediate and direct subjective experience, although it may also be experienced indirectly as feedback from the other readouts. I shall refer to this form of emotion as *affect* from now on. This is what is commonly thought of as emotion. There are many different affects: joy, sorrow, fear, envy, anger, pride, and so on. Affective responses are a subset of emotional responses and refer to subjective feelings such as happiness, sadness, fear, anger, and the like. Emotional responses also include physiological reactions (EI) and facial expressions (EII). I will use the term *affect* for specific feelings that are qualitatively different, and use the more inclusive term *emotion* when that is more appropriate.

This last form of emotion is what I have already referred to as "knowledge by acquaintance," and it serves the function of self-regulation. This subjective experience is read out to the cognitive (rational) system for appraisal, labeling, and self-regulation. The result is rational knowledge by description, which can be symbolically communicated. This last type of knowledge is sequential, analytic, and left brain–oriented, whereas knowledge by acquaintance is more holistic, synthetic, and right brain–oriented. One is immediate knowledge, the other is knowledge based on appraisal.

It is important to note the interaction between the emotional and rational systems of behavior control that is suggested by this explanation. Although an emotional stimulus impinges first on the emotional system, the subjective experience engendered informs the rational-cognitive system and is itself informed in turn through the appraisal of internal and external information. Thus, these systems of behavior control interact and inform each other, leading to goal-directed behavior.

This comprehensive framework accounts for physiological arousal (EI), spontaneous expression (EII), and subjective experience (EIII) as all being parts of the same puzzle. Moreover, the function of reason is seen in a symbiotic relationship with emotion, and it is the interaction of the two systems that determines the consequences of stimuli. The biggest virtue in Buck's model of human behavior, based on emotional-motivational and rational-cognitive systems, is its view of the systems of emotion and reason as working simultaneously and independently and yet interacting with each other.

The following are some questions you may want to think about: Is sexual desire EI, EII, or EIII? Is it a positive emotional response like happiness, joy, elation, pride, or hope or a negative emotional response like fear, anger, disgust, shame, guilt, or sadness? What is the difference between a "positive" and a "negative" emotional response?

THEORIES OF EMOTION

Theories of emotion have variously dealt with the relationship between physiological response, cognition (reason), and emotion. There are two basic schools of thought. Psychophysiological theories see arousal as a necessary and sufficient condition for the primary emotions, which are programmed in their response. On the other hand, psychosocial theories view emotions as malleable states that are defined by cognitive appraisal of the stimulus, so that arousal by itself is a necessary but not sufficient condition for the existence of emotion. As we shall see, these theories may not be incompatible, in that they may more realistically be seen as different aspects of emotional functions.

Whereas psychosocial theories consider the cause of emotion to be an aspect of emotional relationships with others, psychophysiological theories of emotion locate the cause primarily within the individual. The Jamesian theory of emotion (described in the next section) propounded this viewpoint by stating that visceral and skeletal changes produced by stimuli were the source of emotional experience without the mediating influence of cognition. Taking his cue from Darwin's (1872) seminal treatise of emotional expression, Tomkins (1962) posited the facial feedback hypothesis, in which particular facial expressions are typical of each of the primary affects and provide feedback to the viscera, resulting in emotion. The role of cognition or reason in restraining such facial displays for social purposes has been raised in criticism of such a view of emotion that is involuntary and independent of reason.

Early Psychophysiological Theories

At the end of the last century, William James and Carl Lange, working independently, propounded a view that has come to be known as the James-Lange Theory. The theory stated that visceral and skeletal muscle changes produced emotion without the intervention of cognition (understanding) of the emotion. These physiological changes, in other words, completely constitute emotion. Cannon (1927) critiqued the notion that the viscera[1] were the source of emotions and instead attempted, quite wrongly it turned out, to establish the "thalamic theory" (i.e., that the thalamus is the center for emotional experience). Cannon showed that when the viscera are removed, emotion still persists, and also that artificially induced visceral changes do not always produce emotion. In general, he

---

[1] The **viscera** refer to the internal organs of the body such as the stomach, the liver, and the heart. The **thalamus** is a subdivision of the brain. **Homeostasis** is the body's ability to maintain a balance between internal and external events. Note also that from this point on, I shall sometimes use the word **cognition** to indicate reason or rationality.

argued that the viscera do not account for the variety of emotions and are too slow and diffuse to be the center for emotional experiences. Instead, he proposed the "emergency theory" in which bodily sensations serve to adapt us to the environment and, thus, maintain homeostasis by preparing the body to defend itself through a "fight-or-flight" response.

Facial Feedback Theory

Taking his cue from Darwin's seminal treatise on emotional expression, Silvan Tomkins (1962) posited the "facial feedback hypothesis." He argued that variations in the "density of neural firing" from the central nervous system activate the skin and facial muscles and provide feedback to the viscera, resulting in emotion. Particular facial expressions were also considered to be typical of each of the primary affects. Although there is a lack of evidence to suggest that facial feedback causes emotion, Ekman and Freisen (1975) have found evidence to support the other notion that specific affects are associated with universal facial expressions.

Schachter and Singer's Self-Attribution Theory

Whereas Tomkins's theory asserted that emotions are involuntary and independent of cognition, Schachter and Singer (1962) presented a "self-attribution theory" of emotion in which emotion is a function of both physiological arousal and cognitive appraisal of the reasons for arousal. Using epinephrine-induced states, they showed that cognitions are used to label unexplained arousal states. Both behavioral and self-report measures in their study showed that subjects, in the same unexplained arousal state, experienced very disparate emotions (anger and euphoria) according to the situational cues provided to them by confederates in the study. They argued that subjects felt a need to explain and understand their bodily feelings and used cognitive appraisal of the environment to label these feelings.

Psychosocial Theories

Psychosocial theories of emotion (Averill, 1980; deRivera, 1984; Mandler 1982) describe the reciprocal relationship between emotion and the social environment. Emotion is based on social interaction (not automatic arousal) and itself defines the interaction and the relationship. In fact, emotion is viewed *as* emotional relationships, because "We are always in some emotional relationship with others" (deRivera, 1984, p. 142). Such theories are cognition or reason driven, because the environment has to be appraised in order to understand the social situation and, thus, arrive at an emotion. Emotion, in these cases, cannot be predicted from any environmental stimulus alone, because the outcome also is dependent on personality traits and the social relationship between the persons involved. Accordingly, arousal is a necessary but not sufficient condition for emotion, and it is the individual's rational ability to control the interaction that determines the emotion.

Among contemporary theories of emotion there are, thus, two schools of thought. Psychosocial theories (deRivera, Averill, Lazarus, Mandler) are driven by the primacy of cognitions, because the environment has to be appraised in order to understand the social situation and, thus, arrive at an emotion. Emotion is based on social interaction and not on automatic physiological arousal. Psychophysiological theories of emotion, on the other hand, take their cue from Cannon's theory, in which cognition is not a necessary condition for emotion and a stimulus can independently cause objective experience.

What difference do you think this makes in marketing or advertising? What does it matter whether a stimulus leads to emotion indirectly via cognition or if emotion is caused directly by a stimulus?

Lazarus and Zajonc

This debate is also the source of the famous Lazarus-Zajonc controversy. To Lazarus (1984), cognitive cues presented along with the stimulus can determine the nature of the physiological response, and people must understand the emotion in order to experience it. Zajonc (1980), on the other hand, presented Japanese ideographs to subjects and demonstrated that people can have "preferences without inferences." Based on his previous work on "mere exposure" effects, Zajonc (1980) showed that people develop preferences based on familiarity with the stimulus, independent of recognition of the stimulus. Thus, feelings can be achieved towards an unknown object. This controversy is discussed further in the next chapter.

BRINGING IT TOGETHER

As we have seen before in this chapter, Buck (1988) integrates and reconciles all these theories by depicting various forms of emotions. To Buck, emotion serves as a read-out mechanism that carries information about motivational systems and is a continuous and everpresent expression of motivational states. This readout serves three different functions and takes three different emotion forms (EI, EII, EIII) as discussed earlier.

Knowledge by description is sequential, analytic, and left brain–oriented, whereas knowledge by acquaintance is more holistic, synthetic, and right brain–oriented. One is immediate knowledge; the other is based on appraisal. One is syncretic cognition, the other is analytic cognition. Thus, as referred to earlier, Zajonc and Lazarus are both dealing with "cognitions," but of a different type. These are processes described by both Bertrand Russell (1912) and William James (1890)—the processes of knowledge by description and knowledge by acquaintance. Lazarus and

Zajonc are both correct, because they are describing two different processes, both of which are incorporated in the human system.

The conflicting findings of emotion studies are thus reconciled in a comprehensive framework that accounts for physiological arousal, spontaneous expression, and subjective experience as all being parts of the same puzzle. Moreover, the function of reason is seen in an independent yet interactive relationship with emotion and it is the interaction of the two systems that determines the consequences of stimuli. (In fact, Buck adds a third dimension in terms of the developmental history of the individual that concerns past relevant learning that may affect the way a stimulus is apprehended.) Cannon's theory of direct emotional experience, Tomkins's facial feedback hypothesis, and Schachter and Singer's "attribution" theory of emotion are incorporated into one model of human behavior. The process and not the parts is seen.

THE SOURCE OF AFFECTS

What, then, are these emotions? Where do they come from and how do they occur? We know that the biological system consists of different subsystems or levels (cognitions, learned information, affects, drives, instincts, and reflexes) that occur simultaneously and interact. The sources of affect, however, still confound us. Research that attempts to link psychophysiology to consumer behavior has provided conflicting views. Some subscribe to "left brain, right brain" processing, some to the "front-back" dichotomy, and yet another would locate the origin of emotions in a limbic region. There is considerable opinion to suggest that the right hemisphere of the brain is the non-verbal, musical, and intuitive side, while the left hemisphere is the seat of the verbal and the analytical (Hansen, 1981). These differences, however, may be more of degree than of kind and both hemispheres have some roles in the processing of language and music, for instance.

The next section looks at the sources of affect in the human brain and traces our evolutionary heritage in this area. In particular, I will describe MacLean's theory of the triune brain which presents multiple sources of affect in the brain. I will also describe some research results at the end of the chapter which demonstrate that MacLean's theory may have some interesting implications for advertising and promotional strategies.

THE TRIUNE BRAIN

According to MacLean (1990; 1973), the brain has evolved in a series of stages and today there are essentially three brain structures that are interconnected and represent a "triune" brain (see Figure 1.2). The first of

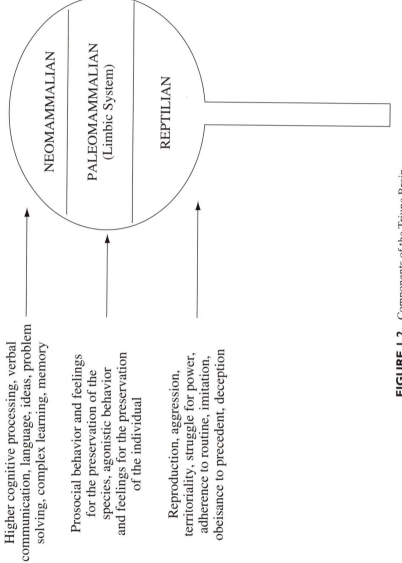

NEOMAMMALIAN

PALEOMAMMALIAN
(Limbic System)

REPTILIAN

Higher cognitive processing, verbal
communication, language, ideas, problem
solving, complex learning, memory

Prosocial behavior and feelings
for the preservation of the
species, agonistic behavior
and feelings for the preservation
of the individual

Reproduction, aggression,
territoriality, struggle for power,
adherence to routine, imitation,
obeisance to precedent, deception

FIGURE 1.2   Components of the Triune Brain.

these structures is the reptilian brain (reticular formation, basal ganglia, and midbrain) that governs such basic behavior as reproduction, aggression, territoriality, etc. The second brain structure is the paleomammalian formation (limbic system) found in mammals, which guides pro-social behavior for the preservation of the species and also agnostic behavior for the preservation of the individual. The third and most recent structure is the neomammalian formation (neocortex and thalamic structures) and its primary functions are in the realm of higher cognitive processing, including verbal communication, language, ideas, problem solving, complex learning, and memory. Importantly, these structures interplay and represent a "whole" that is greater than the sum of its parts.

To cite MacLean (1990, pp. 8–9),

> . . . the human forebrain has evolved and expanded to its great size while retaining the features of three basic evolutionary formations that reflect an ancestral relationship to reptiles, early mammals, and recent mammals. Radically different in chemistry and structure and in an evolutionary sense countless generations apart, the three neural assemblies constitute a hierarchy of three-brains-in-one, a triune brain. . . . the three evolutionary formations might be imagined as three interconnected biological computers, with each having its own special intelligence, its own subjectivity, its own sense of time and space, and its own memory, motor, and other functions. . . . If the three formations are pictured as intermeshing and functioning together as a triune brain, it makes it evident that they cannot be completely autonomous, but does not deny their capacity for operating somewhat independently. . . . the exchange of information among the three brain types means that each derives a greater amount of information than if it were operating alone.

The reptilian brain is the oldest of the three brains and in the earliest reptiles (therapsids) it governed such instinctual behavior as territoriality, hunting, homing, mating, and the creation of social hierarchies. The reptilian counterpart of the human brain is still considered to influence us in our selection of leaders, our love of hunting, our sexual preferences, and even our choice of profession. MacLean also enumerates certain types of basic behavior that derives from our ancestral, evolutionary heritage: struggle for power, adherence to routine, imitation, obeisance to precedent, and deception. Interestingly, these are the same depictions that are often cited as the quintessential "unintended" maladies of advertising (Pollay, 1986).

Whereas the reptilian brain "programmes stereotyped behaviors according to instructions based on ancestral learning and ancestral memories" (MacLean, 1973, p. 8), the paleomammalian or old mammalian portion of the brain, or the limbic system, functions in the experience of emotions and feelings. The development of the limbic cortex constitutes an evolution in brain structures as the result of a transition from reptiles to mammals, and thereby a transition to behaviors associated with nursing, maternal care, and parenting. In general, circuits involving the septal area in the brain are involved in the experience of pro-social feelings associated with behaviors conducive to the preservation of the species. In contrast, circuits involving the area of the amygdala in the limbic cortex are concerned with individualistic feelings such as fear and anger, which are associated with self-preservation and self-protection. MacLean considers such feelings to represent "general affects" and he uses the term *affect* for emotional experience while reserving the word *emotion* for emotional expression.

According to MacLean, the reptilian and paleomammalian formations play an enhanced role in "prosematic" (nonverbal) communication and behavior. On the other hand, the neomammalian brain is the realm of verbal communication, language, problem solving, and higher order learning. Thus, MacLean argues that emotion and reason, though complimentary, may occur independently because they derive from different brain structures. The neocortex is largest in human beings and allows the translation of internal states (affects, etc.) into verbal representation through the use of formalized language or any other symbolic communication that uses a system of rules to derive meaning. This "third" brain allows for the creation, transmission, and preservation of ideas, information, and culture. In its orientation, it is more attuned to the outside world.

The Triune Brain

MacLean's contribution in understanding the development and evolution of the human brain can also be viewed as a reconciliation of the long-standing controversy between typological and dimensional approaches to affect. One school of thought (Ekman & Friesen, 1975; Plutchik, 1980) has viewed affects as qualitatively different states such as anger, fear, happiness, and so on. The other (Mehrabian & Russell, 1974) has been inclined to see affect in dimensional continuums of strong/weak, pleasant/unpleasant, and reward/punishment. MacLean's "triune" explanation reveals that both systems exist in the human brain. For instance, the older reptilian structures in the brain do possess dimensions of arousal and reward/punishment. At the same time, as discussed earlier, newer structures have evolved over time and the limbic system contains areas that are associated with happiness, fear, and anger. Thus, both approaches are partially correct and the theory of the "triune brain" incorporates both.

Reptilian Behaviors

MacLean (1990) describes six general forms of basic behavior among reptiles that have striking similarities to the behaviors that are encouraged, aided, and abetted in modern day advertising. These behaviors arise out of motivations emanating from the reptilian brain and hark back millions of years to the reptiles (therapsids) who roamed the world (long before the dinosaurs) in the Triassic age.

1. *Routinization*. This is characterized by "the regular round the clock, temporal sequencing of behavior" (p. 143). This daily temporal aspect distinguishes routinization from the behaviors of repetition and reenactment that are also described later in this list. Routines include master routines during the day (sleeping, waking, defecation, basking, etc.) and subroutines, which refer to typical behaviors during the day by individual reptiles. Subroutines (sleeping in the same place every day) develop from a precedent being established. Once an activity is found to be acceptable, a precedent is set and a subroutine emerges. Younger reptiles have been seen to follow a subroutine established by a more experienced reptile. When subroutines develop a rigid structure in pattern and time, they become rituals. Reptiles (and people?!) are slaves to routine, precedent, and ritual. This obeisance to precedent may have important survival value in terms of safety in taking a familiar route to work, for example.

Do consumers have routines, subroutines, and rituals? When I was growing up, I remember my mother would go shopping every day (routine). And she had a typical favored route in the bazaar that she frequented (subroutine). Then there was the daily ritualistic complaint of the produce purchased the previous day and the bargaining for the produce for the day. Sometimes when she was unwell, she would send me and I would find myself taking the same routes and even attempting the same ritualistic bargaining techniques. With much less success, of course!

Modern day consumers also have subroutines or "schemas" in their minds when they go to the supermarket. What are your own shopping patterns when you go to the grocery store? Also, do you routinely buy and use brands that you have found to be acceptable? Brand loyalty is all about establishing precedence and subsequent routine purchasing, is it not? Certain acts become established as rituals and incorporated into the daily routine of reptiles and, it would appear, consumers! Quite often these are passed on from generation to generation, as depicted in past ads for Johnson and Johnson's baby powder, among other ads.

2. *Isopraxic behavior*. This refers to performing or acting in a like manner. To cite MacLean (1990), "When two territorial male lizards of the same species are responding to one another with challenge displays, they are essentially engaged in isopraxic behavior, i.e., behaving in a like manner" (p. 144). This is not quite the same as "imitation" because it is not necessarily learned behavior. In the language of this book, it is spontaneous communication that is biologically inherited and shared between members of the same species.

Interestingly, MacLean also provides us with examples of group and mass isopraxic behavior in human beings such as mass migrations, mass rallies, and mass adoption by millions of people of fads and fashions. People collect beanie babies all over the world. This is isopraxic behavior.

3. *Tropistic behavior.* We can think of this as fixed action patterns or our innate or unborn inclinations to stimuli like a nonverbal sign, a color, or a movement. In biology, the turning of a plant towards the sun is a tropism. Among lizards, different colors have been noted to promote differences in aggressive and courtship displays.

Can you think of instinctive responses by consumers that have implications for advertising and consumer behavior? For instance, what are some visual stimuli that get immediate attention in advertising? Once again, this is spontaneous communication of nonverbal stimuli that results in abiding behavioral patterns among humans. This is, of course, especially important in global advertising campaigns because we are discussing human and not culturally learned behavior.

While writing this chapter, I could not help thinking about my strange feeling towards snakes. I am terrified of the creatures, yet there is a compulsion to see more of them and learn more about them. Every time I am in the zoo, I take five steps forward to the reptile house and then come five steps right back. I watch the movie *Anaconda* avidly, but with a strange mixture of fear and anticipation, anxiety and excitement. Could it be that something very deep and personal in us is still drawn irresistibly but powerfully and attractively to our evolutionary heritage in the reptilian world?

4. *Repetitious behavior.* This is defined as "the repetitive performance of a certain act" (MacLean, 1990, pp. 146–147) or the repeated performance over and over again of a specific act, such as a display. The attention of others may be drawn by the number of displays, in addition to the magnitude of the display. Such repetition may also have a certain attraction for us, if we are to believe the advertising claim by AT&T that "the more you hear, the better we sound."

5. *Reenactment behavior.* This behavior "applies to a repeated performance in which a number of actions are meaningfully related" (MacLean, 1990, p. 147). Female green turtles on the coast of Brazil migrate 1,400 miles every 2–3 years to lay their eggs on Ascension Island, which is only 5 miles wide.

Generation after generation, people reenact sequences of acts on a single day or at periodic intervals ranging from days to years. Anniversaries, birthdays, Father's Day, Mother's Day, Armed Forces Day, Groundhog Day! A great deal of modern marketing is devoted to facilitating these reenactments for consumers through products and services.

6. *Deceptive behavior*. This is the most essential behavior for survival. In reptiles, it is involved in obtaining the necessities of life like a home, food (deceptive behavior is needed to get prey), and mating, in which deceptive signals are often sent! One cannot help thinking of human mating games and the appeal of a Dry Idea ad, which says, "Never let them see you sweat."

Other reptilian behaviors that may have special ramifications for the marketing of ideas, goods, and services include the struggle for power, the establishment of a social hierarchy, and the formation of social groups. This brings to mind our selection and acceptance of leaders in human communities and countries. Grooming, courtship, mating, and breeding are also reptilian behaviors that have their human counterparts, and I do not have to point out to you how many ads depict the successful culmination of these behaviors through advertised products and services.

I must also point out the similarities between reptiles and humans in the establishment, marking, and defense of territory. These are innate responses that are not necessarily learned behaviors from watching other humans. Their roots may lie much deeper. MacLean refers to territoriality as a "demonstrated determination to protect a particular piece of ground" (MacLean, 1990, p. 229). This striving for territory also marks the human struggle for dominance that we see mirrored everywhere in nature. Note that among reptiles (as in political advertising) it is sometimes the number of displays (ad repetition) and not the size of the display (a single ad) that decides the winner in the fight (polls). Note also, as MacLean points out, that the lizard in his own territory has a home ground advantage over larger combatants just like a politician is confident of winning in his home state!

The human, animal, and reptilian struggle for territoriality is especially important because it is a necessary first step to courtship, mating, and breeding. The homeowner has a decided advantage in finding a mate and raising a family. Thus, these behaviors are crucial for the preservation and support of the species. Consequently, we are programmed at birth (and not only as a result of socialization) to be mindful of our "space." Children with little or no instructions have been seen to establish territorial domains. Throughout our lives, we establish territories in our homes and our jobs, and we vigilantly protect these areas! MacLean points out how much legal material exists regarding land and possessions.

Contrast the reptilian behaviors we have discussed with mammalian-type behaviors such as nursing, maternal care, parenting, play, and audiovocal communication. Some of these have no counterparts in the reptilian world. The addition of these mammalian behaviors correspond to the development of the limbic system in the brain and bring with them an enhanced realm of feelings and sentiments that promote self-preservation, the preservation of the species, and a sense of personal identity. Contrast these mammalian behaviors, in turn, with the neomammalian functions arising out of the neocortex and the thalamic regions of the brain, the culmination of which is greatest in the human brain. The neomammalian brain has extensive connections to the sensory systems and, therefore, appears to be primarily oriented to the external world. It also affords us with the capacity for problem solving, learning, and memory of details. Its capacity for verbal communication helps to promote and preserve ideas and information and this, in turn, promotes the transmission and preservation of culture.

There has been considerable work (Batra & Ray, 1986; Edell & Burke, 1987; Holbrook & Batra, 1987) in advertising research suggesting a range of affective and cognitive effects, but scant attention has been paid to the reptilian brain, which, as we have discussed, may play a significant role in the advertising process. Consider, for instance, MacLean's (1990) detailed descriptions of such reptilian behaviors as adherence to routine, reenactment, imitation, repetition, struggle for power, mating, territoriality, tropistic behavior, and deception. Also consider the relevance of these behaviors to advertising appeals such as "never let them see you sweat" (deception), "think of it as caviar for the power hungry" (power), "tell her you'll marry her all over again" (reenactment), "did you DQ today?" (routine), and "the more you hear, the better it sounds" (repetition). The list is almost endless. The exhortations of a large body of advertising are direct appeals to reptilian behaviors.

Further, the inclusion of the reptilian dimension substantially increases the range of affective responses that are usually considered in marketing and advertising. In accordance with MacLean's (1990) "triune" theory of the brain, it is suggested here that affective outcomes in advertising represent the workings of the "old mammalian" (limbic system) as well as the "reptilian" portions of the brain. The dimension of positive affect, composed of such elements as happiness, affiliation, and the like, is generally identified with the septal area of the limbic system and conforms to the "social" emotional systems that are concerned with the preservation of the species. Another dimension of affect composed of anger, fear, and the like is associated with the amygdala in the limbic system and conforms to the "individualistic" emotional systems concerned with self-preservation. A third dimension composed of sex, aggression, and power conforms to the older, "reptilian" structure in the brain made up of the brain stem, midbrain, and basal ganglia. Such a multidimensional and hierarchical view of specific emotion systems (see Buck, 1999 for a comprehensive description and analysis), grounded in current neurophysiological theories of the brain, offers significant potential for understanding the structure and sources of affect and its impact on persuasion in general.

RESEARCH RESULTS

The CASC Scale

A study was conducted to develop a scale that measured multidimensional elements of emotional and rational responses to advertising. The study showed that emotional and rational outcomes (syncretic and analytic cognitions), as measured by the CASC (Communication Analytic and Syncretic Cognitions) scale, are characterized along the dimensions of a "triune brain" (MacLean 1973, 1990). It also suggested that the multidimensional elements of the CASC scale are directly linked to measures of advertising effectiveness such as "liking" and "buying."

Specifically, the following research issues were investigated:

1. Do certain thoughts and feelings repeatedly occur on exposure to advertising? Are these constant across different samples of individuals and different samples of ads? Do these remain the same when both individuals and ads are used as the units of analysis? Are these constant across different media?
2. Do these responses conform to the dimensions postulated by brain theory?
3. Do such responses affect individuals' evaluation of ads?

The CASC scale is based on MacLean's "triune" theory of the brain and consists of items that investigate rational and emotional responses elicited by advertising. It is a multidimensional scale consisting of four subscales; of these, one subscale contains rational items, while the other three subscales ask for emotional responses on the dimensions of reptilian, pro-social, and individualistic feelings. CASC is a seven-point paper and pencil scale anchored at two ends by "Not At All" and "A Lot." The general form of the scale is "Did the ad make you think/feel . . .". In all, there are 16 items, 4 for each subscale.

The items in the scale were validated in two different studies—the first using individuals as the unit of analysis, the second using advertisements as the unit of analysis. In the first study, the scale was validated using multiple samples of individuals. In the second study, a sample of 240 advertisements was used. Reliabilities and dimensions were replicated across different subjects, different ads, and different media, and using both individuals and advertisements as the units of analysis. The predictive validity of the scale was also tested against traditional measures of advertising effectiveness. A 16-item scale emerged that measured advertising responses in terms of reptilian, pro-social, individualistic, and analytic dimensions.

Table 1.1 shows the results of principal components analysis on the data set using ads as the units of analysis. The results are provided for the total sample of ads (N = 240) and also separately for TV (N = 120) and magazine (N = 120) subsamples of ads. In all three cases, only four factors emerged with eigenvalues greater than 1.0. In fact, the results are very similar when broken down by media. Notice also that, with only one exception ("fear"), all the items load .50 or higher on the appropriate dimensions. Moreover, none of the items crossload higher than .41 on a second factor. Additionally, the four factors accounted for 74.8% of the variance in the total sample, 74.4% of the variance in the television subsample, and 77.5% of the variance in the magazine subsample.

TABLE 1.1   Principal Components Solutions of Ad Level Analyses

	Factor 1			Factor 2			Factor 3			Factor 4		
	TS	TV	MG	TS	TV	MG	TS	TV	MG	TS	TV	MG
Cognition												
diffs. with comp.	**.91**	**.91**	**.90**	−.09	−.16	−.02	.02	.09	−.05	−.04	−.04	−.11
pros & cons	**.96**	**.96**	**.95**	−.02	−.07	.07	.03	.02	.03	.04	.00	.01
arguments	**.93**	**.92**	**.92**	.00	−.09	.14	−.02	−.03	.00	.11	.12	.02
think of facts	**.93**	**.93**	**.90**	.02	−.02	.10	.00	−.04	.04	−.02	.04	−.15
Positive Affect												
happy	−.24	−.19	−.16	**.76**	**.71**	**.84**	.12	.18	.07	−.20	−.04	−.10
proud	−.04	−.13	.15	**.85**	**.88**	**.77**	.28	.26	.35	−.03	−.03	−.07
hope	.02	−.10	.23	**.85**	**.87**	**.79**	.29	.25	.35	.00	.08	.01
affiliation	.10	.06	.21	**.83**	**.79**	**.83**	.20	.28	.14	−.05	.02	−.01
Reptilian												
envy	−.02	−.09	.07	.32	.33	.28	**.71**	**.69**	**.70**	.03	−.16	.24
aggressive	.05	.05	.05	.11	.17	.06	**.86**	**.82**	**.87**	.07	.03	.12
sexy	−.12	−.06	−.19	.13	.09	.20	**.78**	**.79**	**.76**	.06	−.02	.10
power	.20	.21	.21	.40	.41	.40	**.74**	**.69**	**.79**	.05	.04	.05
Negative Affect												
fear	.18	.00	.47	.19	.12	.16	−.01	−.15	.28	**.47**	**.58**	**.30**
anger	.01	.04	.07	−.01	−.08	−.02	.11	.00	.29	**.88**	**.89**	**.84**
disgust	−.09	.00	−.08	−.08	−.27	.08	.07	.07	.09	**.86**	**.81**	**.89**
irritated	−.02	.20	−.11	−.27	−.53	.07	.04	.09	.04	**.77**	**.56**	**.88**
% variance	27.7	31.3	32.7	23.2	22.0	22.6	15.9	13.1	14.6	7.9	7.9	7.6

Abbreviations: TS = total sample; TV = television; MG = magazine

Predictive Validity

In order to demonstrate the predictive validity of the CASC scale, factor scores for the four factors in the aggregative data set (ads as the unit of analysis) were saved and these factors were used as independent variables in a regression analysis that included measures of advertising effectiveness as dependent variables. Multicollinearity among the predictors was avoided because principal components analysis extracts factors as orthogonal dimensions. The dependent variables were also aggregated responses that had been solicited along with analytic and syncretic cognitions (rational and emotional responses) in Study Two. Specifically, these were:

1. Three evaluation items from past studies (Burton & Lichtenstein, 1988; Edell & Burke, 1987) which, when summed, formed a positive evaluation scale (alpha = .952). The items consisted of: "Was the ad convincing," "Was the ad persuasive," "Was the ad effective." Responses were recorded on a seven point scale with "Not At All" and "A Lot" at the endpoints.
2. Two single item responses that served to measure "liking" and "buying." The items (also on a seven-point scale) were "How much did you like the ad?" and "Was the ad effective in leading you to buy the product?"

Likability has repeatedly been identified by practitioners to be a strong determinant of brand and commercial success (McCarthy, 1991), and ad effectiveness in terms of buying the product is clearly a worthwhile objective. Past research (Batra & Ray, 1986; Edell & Burke, 1987; Holbrook & Batra, 1987) has demonstrated that emotional responses are related to attitudinal measures of ad effectiveness similar to those used in this study and, accordingly, the multidimensional elements of the CASC scale can also be expected to predict ad effectiveness.

Analytic, pro-social, and individualistic were all significantly related ($p < .001$) to positive evaluation, and individualistic, understandably, had a negative beta weight (.172). Pro-social and analytic were the best predictors, with beta weights of .611 and .524, respectively. Reptilian was also positively related to positive evaluation at the .05 level. Together the four predictors explained an impressively large amount of variance in positive evaluation (R square = .685).

Only the three syncretic cognitive (emotional) subscales were related to liking, with pro-social and individualistic serving as large and significant ($p < .001$) predictors. Pro-social was positively related (beta = .663) to liking while individualistic was negatively related (beta = $-.326$) to liking, and once again, the independent variables accounted for a sizeable amount of explained variance in the dependent variable (R square = .554).

In the case of the reptilian factor, further analysis using orthogonal polynomials suggested that although the factor in its linear form was only weakly related to both positive evaluation and liking, there was a significant nonlinear relationship of sufficient magnitude between reptilian and positive evaluation (beta = .229, p < .01) and reptilian and liking (beta = .282, p < .001). It would appear that reptilian emotions (sex, aggression, envy, and power) have a special association with measures of ad effectiveness: They are most effective in moderate amounts. Too much or too little leads to a less effective ad.

Interestingly, analytic, which was not related to liking, was related to buying (p < .001) and had a sizeable beta weight (.491). Pro-social and individualistic also made significant (p < .001) contributions to the prediction of buying, with pro-social being a specially large predictor (beta = .456). Reptilian was not related to buying at the .05 level in either linear or nonlinear forms. Together, the predictors explained 47.5% of the variance in buying.

In sum, pro-social affects were always strongly and positively related to positive evaluation, liking, and buying. Individualistic affects were negatively related to all three dependent variables. Reptilian affects were curvilinearly related to positive evaluation and liking but had no significant relationship with buying. Analytic cognition was related to positive evaluation and buying but was not significantly related to liking. Additionally, the four predictors explained a large portion of the variance in all three dependent variables. Overall, the results of the regression analysis strongly confirm that the four dimensions of the CASC scale are capable of predicting selected measures of advertising effectiveness.

The evidence garnered provides a new perspective on the study of emotion and reason in advertising, and the CASC scale has the added virtue of being grounded in accepted scientific evidence on the workings of the human brain. Past studies in advertising have used different emotional items based on various theoretical frameworks; there is no commonly accepted scale for the measurement of emotional and rational outcomes and, consequently, little replication of effects. This study suggests that certain thoughts and feelings are repeatedly and consistently evoked by advertising and that these conform to the functioning of certain brain structures that have evolved during the course of evolution (Buck, 1984, 1988).

Discussion

Despite the widespread use of emotional responses in advertising, the range of rational and emotional responses has not yet been operationalized into a *practical* multicomponent scale that is reliable and valid (see also Chaudhuri, 2005). The present study attempts to fill this void with a scale that is relatively short, yet encompasses a variety of emotional responses that have been established in brain research. These results converge with past research, notably that of Edell and Burke (1987), who also found three feelings dimensions in emotional responses to advertising. However, the findings reported in this study also draw on cognitions as an additional dimension and, most importantly, they mark a theoretical advancement in our *understanding* of emotional and rational responses in terms of systems that correspond to actual brain systems. Rather than naming emotional responses in terms of "positive," "negative," "upbeat," or "warm," dimensions, our understanding is enriched when we begin to view these phenomena as part of our evolutionary heritage and critical to the preservation of both the individual and the species. It is seen that these emotional and rational responses are repetitively and reliably evoked by advertising and that they are consistent across both individual and aggregative levels of analysis. Further, the findings have been replicated over different samples of individuals and ads and across different media. Additionally, it is shown that the components of the scale are strongly predictive of certain measures of ad effectiveness.

The results indicate that advertising creates both product knowledge and positive, desirable, pro-social feelings. Further, such responses predict positive and favorable evaluations of advertisements and may even be effective in creating sales. On the other hand, the results also indicate that certain negative feelings such as anger, disgust, and fear also occur, and in sufficient quantity to deserve our special consideration. Moreover, these last consequences are undesirable from both ethical *and* effectiveness points of view. Although there may be special circumstances where "fear appeals" or "anger appeals" are effective, our data show that these affects are clearly predictive of a *negative* evaluation of advertisements and they are *negatively related* to ads being liked or products being purchased.

Thus, it is recommended that advertisers assess their campaigns in terms of the dimensions suggested in the CASC scale. "Emotional" ads are widely used today and large sums of money are appropriated for "image" campaigns, but advertisers may not be completely cognizant of the range of emotional experiences that their ads evoke. The simplicity of the CASC scale makes it useful for conducting large scale testing of cognitive responses and advertising effectiveness. The scale can be used to aggregate responses and assign scores to ads or it can be used to assess individual-level processing of ads. Further, it can be used for ads in both print and electronic media and for a variety of consumer products. Finally, the scale can be used to test ads with vastly different advertising strategies because it has been validated in a sample of 240 ads that contained sex, humor, animation, patriotism, status, fear appeals, family situations, celebrities, animals, typical spokespersons, product demonstrations, comparisons, price appeals, health appeals, and so on.

Limitations and Future Research

The CASC scale does not claim to measure the entire range of human emotional experience. The effort has been to introduce a practical scale that conforms to certain dimensions of analytic and syncretic cognitive activity. There may well be other dimensions that future research will uncover. For instance, the results reveal that "fear" may at times constitute a separate dimension. More work needs to be done using fear appeals and other closely related indicators of fear such as anxiety, foreboding, and apprehension. Also, the analytic dimension has been constrained by the choice of indicators to largely reflect responses to brand differentiation strategies in ads. There may well be a "newness" dimension (see Coulson, 1989) in analytic thoughts that is elicited by ads for new products, an area not specifically investigated in our studies.

This work has also been confined to ads for consumer goods; it is feasible that advertising for ideas, services, industrial, and business-to-business products may evoke other responses of special interest to these areas of marketing. For example, guilt, shame, and other related "social affects" described by Buck (1988) may be of special interest to charitable organizations that solicit donations in their ads.

Further replication of the scale must also be conducted among populations of particular interest to advertisers. The student population used in the studies reported here are admittedly not representative of the universe of consumers. However, because emotional and rational responses constitute basic, human, psychological responses it is likely that replications in other populations will reproduce similar results. Replications that extend this work to other samples will increase the generalizability of the scale.

"The CASC Scale"

This questionnaire asks for your reactions to different ads. After you see each ad, give your responses to the ad. Then wait for the next ad. And so on. Remember, this is not a test and there are no correct answers, only honest ones. Be sincere. Some of the questions ask for the feelings the ad may have aroused in you. Other questions ask about your thoughts during the ad. Use a check on the seven-point scale to show the *extent* of your feelings/thoughts.

	NOT AT ALL VERY MUCH
	(1)(2)(3)(4)(5)(6)(7)
Did the ad make you feel happy?	:__:__:__:__:__:__:
Did the ad make you think of real differences between the brand and its competitors?	:__:__:__:__:__:__:
Did the ad make you feel sexy?	:__:__:__:__:__:__:
Did the ad make you feel afraid?	:__:__:__:__:__:__:
Did the ad make you think of the pros or cons of the brand?	:__:__:__:__:__:__:
Did the ad make you feel hopeful?	:__:__:__:__:__:__:
Did the ad make you feel angry?	:__:__:__:__:__:__:
Did the ad make you think of arguments for using or not using the brand?	:__:__:__:__:__:__:
Did the ad make you feel disgusted?	:__:__:__:__:__:__:
Did the ad make you feel a sense of power?	:__:__:__:__:__:__:
Did the ad make you think of facts about the brand?	:__:__:__:__:__:__:
Did the ad make you feel envious?	:__:__:__:__:__:__:
Did the ad make you feel a sense of affiliation?	:__:__:__:__:__:__:
Did the ad make you feel aggressive?	:__:__:__:__:__:__:
Did the ad make you feel irritated?	:__:__:__:__:__:__:
Did the ad make you feel proud?	:__:__:__:__:__:__:

2

EMOTION AND REASON

". . . and blest are those
Whose blood and judgment are so well comingled,
That they are not a pipe for fortune's finger
To sound what stop she pleases. Give me the man
That is not passion's slave, and I will wear him
In my heart's core, ay, in my heart of heart,
As I do thee."

(Hamlet, III, 2)

"Oh judgment, thou art fled to brutish beasts,
And men have lost their reason."

(Julius Caesar, III, 2)

The interplay of emotion and reason in the human mind has interested poets, psychologists, and philosophers. William Shakespeare, Sigmund Freud, and Bertrand Russell, to name just a few, have all pondered the nature of the relationships that govern the struggle between these archetypal aspects of the human psyche. Do they work together or separately? Under what conditions is one more dominant than the other? What are the sources in the human brain that lead to greater emotionality and greater rationality in people? And what are the sources in the outside environment that provoke, stimulate, and engender particular thoughts and feelings?

The answers to some of these questions are also of some significance to those in the persuasion "business." For instance, marketing and advertising practitioners have always used emotional and rational appeals in promoting ideas, goods, and services. A Hallmark television commercial draws heavily on emotional devices like nostalgia, family affection, and children. A print advertisement for a mid-sized sedan uses both emotional and rational appeals in the slogan, "Drive Safely." This chapter addresses the interplay of emotion and reason, their relative merits and uses in advertising and media planning, and their role in product positioning.

THE NATURE OF AFFECT

Although feelings are intrinsic to human beings, the study of affect (Emotion III) in specifically market persuasion situations has only recently begun. There was some interest during the 1950s and 1960s regarding emotional exploitation in advertising, but, in general, the role of affect in marketing applications did not begin to be studied until the early 1980s. This was probably because affects or feelings are difficult to assess because they are not amenable to control and evaluation as are the more often mentioned thoughtful, rational processes.

Since then, the marketing literature has established that affective executions of ads lead to more favorable attitudes for the product, because the liking for an advertisement gets conditioned onto the brand itself and becomes part of the attitude to the brand (Gorn, 1982). This may take place in the total absence of rational beliefs and product attributes. Some social psychologists disagree with this and consider affects to occur after rational processing has taken place (i.e., affects are dependent on reason because they occur after and as a result of rational processing). On the other hand, work done in the field by Zajonc (1980) bears out the independent nature of affective judgments. Zajonc has shown that affects may indeed precede rational processing. Moreland and Zajonc (1977) exposed subjects to Japanese ideographs and recorded a variety of recognition and liking judgments. Experimental evidence was obtained to show that reliable affective discrimination (like-dislike ratings) can be made in the total absence of a rational process such as recognition memory.

Characteristics of the affective component as described by Zajonc (1980) are:

- *Affects are primary.* They govern our first response to the environment and determine out subsequent relations with it. Very often we delude ourselves that we have arrived at a decision in a rational manner, whereas in reality, the decision has been made on an "I like it" basis. We may justify our choices by various reasons but it is the affective that has proved decisive.
- *Affects are basic.* Affective responses are universal among the animal species, irrespective of language or reason. Affects existed before language was evolved and before rational abilities were developed.
- *Affects are inescapable.* These experiences of affect occur with little control over them on our part. We may control the expression of emotion but we cannot escape the experience itself.
- *Affects are irrevocable.* Once an evaluation is formed on the basis of an affective response, it is not readily revoked. There is permanence to affect as, for example, in the abiding nature of our first impressions of people. Affective judgments are irrevocable because

they "feel" valid and we believe them to be "true." Feelings may then well represent basic reality.

- *Affects implicate the self.* Affects identify the state of the person with relation to the object.
- *Affects are difficult to verbalize.* The communication of affect relies largely on nonverbal channels. Expressions of surprise, anger, delight, and serenity are very similar across cultures.
- *Affects may become separated from content and still remain.* The feelings caused by a book or movie are often readily accessible, though the contents may have been forgotten.

The last point indicates Zajonc's main tenet that affective reactions need not depend on cognition. In the 1977 experiment mentioned before, Moreland and Zajonc showed 20 slides to pairs of subjects for 2 seconds each and at varying frequencies (0, 1, 3, 9, 27). Affect and recognition ratings were then taken. A strong path (.96) from stimulus exposure directly to subjective affect, independent of recognition, was found. Affective reactions to a stimulus may then be acquired by virtue of experience with that stimulus, even if not accompanied by a rational process such as recognition of the stimulus. In contrast to reason, affects are the first reaction to stimuli, are made without perceptual "encoding," and are made with greater confidence and more quickly. Thus it is not necessary to "know" something before liking it. However, all rational cognitions are accompanied by affects despite parallel yet separate and independent systems.

To quote Zajonc (1980, p. 153) on the pervasive nature of emotions, he says, "There are practically no social phenomena that do not implicate affect in some important way. Affect dominates social interaction and it is the major currency in which all social intercourse is transacted." For instance, one cannot meet a person without feeling some inner attraction or revulsion. Affective reactions are thus important because we do not simply see things as they are, but instead, we provide affective interpretations of them (e.g., not just a sunset, but a "beautiful" sunset).

COMPARING EMOTIONAL AND RATIONAL PERSUASION

Emotions can never be wrong. Understanding and the intellect can betray us and prove us wrong, but emotions are always true and real. There can be no doubt about the existence of feeling. This virtue has marketing applications. Consumers can be wrong about their beliefs about a product, but they can have no misconception about their emotional response to a product or advertisement. We, as marketers, may mistake how they feel and consumers themselves may not always reveal their true internal state. Nevertheless, if we can generate feelings, these will be genuine and accurate and, thus, more resistant to competitive claims than a rational belief in the virtues of the product. Rational beliefs about products can be changed by competitors providing "new evidence" in the way of taste tests and the like. It will be much harder to change a consumer's overall affective disposition to a brand. Beliefs are amenable to change; feelings are more resistant.

Buck (1984) makes the same point when he distinguishes between spontaneous communication, which is nonvoluntary, nonpropositional (cannot be false), and nonsymbolic, and signals meaning via a biologically based system, and symbolic communication, which is intentional, propositional, and functions on a socially shared system (such as language) between sender and receiver.

What would it take to change someone's positive feelings of liking towards a brand? A price change? Bad word of mouth from a friend? A single bad experience with the brand? Nonavailability of the brand? None of the above? It would seem, then, that emotions can create long-term brand loyalty, which is the goal of most marketing campaigns. Of course, rational beliefs can lead to repeated buying of the brand as well. However, when you have an emotional commitment to the brand you may also have a superior kind of brand loyalty. Aaker (1991) distinguishes between different types of brand loyalty. Contrast, for example, the car buyer who buys a Beetle because she "loves" it and the buyer who buys a Hyundai because it is cheaper. Whose loyalty could you count on in the future?

Emotions are global. By showing photographs of facial expressions to observers, Ekman and Friesen (1975) identified six widely occurring emotions, usually referred to as the six basic affects: happiness, sadness, fear, anger, surprise, and disgust. Darwin's (1872) seminal book on facial expressions established that such expressions are universal and not cultural. Affects are basic and common across cultures and universal in their signal systems. Thus, affects produce more predictable reactions across consumer segments than cognitive systems, which are different across cultures.

Emotional treatments would thus be preferable to rational treatments for "global" advertising. If you remember that emotional communication is "spontaneous," then this enhances the utility of emotional messages in global persuasion campaigns. Notice how large companies with worldwide operations are developing logos and advertisements that are largely nonverbal and thus easily translated (emotionally) across cultures. Nike has replaced its name with just a swoosh. Coke uses ads with nonspeaking polar bears whose appeal can be "understood" (again, emotionally) in any culture. This emotional language is the new persuasion strategy in global marketing.

Emotions are fundamental. Ray and Batra (1983) state that the affective is the first level of response and governs our subsequent relations with the environment. It primes and makes available the inference rules that favor positive appraisals, because it creates uncritical judgments of a favorable nature. Cognitive defenses are lowered by emotional treatments. Very often, we use rational arguments to justify what we really "feel" like doing. Volvo uses this in the headline of an ad urging Americans to buy the car in Europe because it is cheaper—"How to justify a European vacation." The "real" reason is the pleasure of touring Europe in a new sedan. The justification is the rationality of obtaining a lower price for the car while in Europe.

Emotions are fast, catchy, and memorable. Emotional appeals lead to better attention getting, better processing of information, and better retention in memory (Ray & Batra, 1983). Because these appeals are often (but not always) nonverbal they are also quicker to communicate. A picture speaks faster than a sentence and, once again, this type of "spontaneous" communication has an impact very different and often more complete than that of "symbolic" communication using words.

Emotions are permanent. According to Zajonc (1980), we have little control over affects and once evoked, they are irrevocable. Affects may become separated from content and still remain. We may forget the content of a book, movie, or advertisement, but not the feelings elicited by them. This is especially significant for marketing communications because affective attitudes may, thus, be less conducive to change than cognitive ones. For instance, whereas cognitive brand attitudes can be changed by merely supplying competing information of a more favorable kind (price appeals, etc.), brand attitudes created by affect may be more abiding and even irrevocable because, according to Zajonc, these are also independent of content.

Emotions are independent of rational cognition. Affects do not depend on rational cognitions, whereas all social phenomena involve affects (Zajonc, 1980). Affective reactions may be acquired by virtue of experience with a stimulus, even if not accompanied by a rational message. However, all rational cognitions are accompanied by affects—we do not see an advertisement without interpreting it as a "good" or "bad" ad.

Overall, emotional positioning is inherently superior to positioning your brand only on rational attributes. Your brand's competitors can copy your rational product benefits and say that they "do it better." However, if you have created a long-term emotional image for your brand, your competitors would be foolish to copy it. Think about it. If you used cowboys in a cigarette ad or babies in an automobile tires ad, who would consumers think the ad was for? You would actually be spending your ad dollars to promote Marlboro or Michelin!

Can you think of disadvantages of emotional treatments in advertising? I can think of one—they are more risky in terms of creating a controversy. Think of the Calvin Klein ads, which have been accused of child pornography, or the Benetton ads, which used emotional themes like

AIDS, war, and racism. These are all ads that have stirred negative feelings in people, and the sponsors of these ads have been criticized for poor taste. Will this negativity carry on to sales of the products? Or will the publicity generated by the ads create greater recall of the brands? For instance, the "sleeper effect" might lead us to believe that, over time, people may forget the negative element and just focus on the brand, in which case, they are really discussing an advantage of emotional treatments! However, in general, most companies play it safe and do not actively pursue a strategy of offending people. Emotional treatments using socially sensitive themes are too risky!

Another caveat to remember is that "image" without substance is not likely to work in the long run. Emotional persuasion must be backed up by quality products and services. I think it was Abraham Lincoln who said that "You can fool some of the people all of the time, and all of the people some of the time, but you cannot fool all of the people all of the time." Not that emotional persuasion is the same as "fooling" people. Not at all. But, with most products, you need to satisfy the rational as well as the emotional needs of your consumers.

RESEARCH RESULTS[1]

A Study of the Independence of Emotion and Reason

Purpose of the Study

The subject of the independence of affect from cognition has been a controversial one (Lazarus, 1984; Zajonc, 1980). According to Zajonc, affect can be evoked prior to cognition and it can be independent of cognition. On the other hand, Lazarus has argued that affect is dependent on cognition. Consumer researchers (Anand, Holbrook, & Stephens, 1988; Tsal, 1985) have also contested the notion of the independence of affect. Others (Heath, 1990; Janiszewski, 1988) have continued to espouse the mere exposure (Moreland & Zajonc, 1977) effect through which affect is supposed to obtain its effect independent of recognition.

Most studies have tested affect using generalized affect measurements such as like-dislike ratings. The purpose of this study is to test the independence of affect using qualitatively different types of affects such as prosocial feelings, based on paleocortical (limbic) parts of the brain, and reptilian feelings, based on subcortical areas (MacLean, 1993). Recent brain research shows that certain emotional structures in the brain receive

---

[1] This research is reprinted with permission from the 2004 AMA Winter Educators' Conference Proceedings, published by the American Marketing Association, Chaudhuri, Arjun, 2004, Vol. 15, 286–292.

information independently of the neocortical structures associated with cognition (LeDoux, 1996). Thus, it is possible that different types of affect may function differently in their relationship to cognition. Buck and his colleagues (1988, 1995, 1999) have argued that reptilian emotions involve "raw" sex and aggression whereas prosocial-limbic emotions involve attachment, which serves as the basis for feelings such as love, pride, and pity. Buck and his colleagues have also developed the ARI (Affect, Reason, Involvement) model in which reason and affect combine in different proportions, suggesting that affect is not an undifferentiated concept and that different types of affects may have different relationships with reason or cognition. It may be that both Zajonc and Lazarus are right, depending on which type of affect is in question.

Accordingly, I conducted a study of the independence of affect using both prosocial and reptilian feelings as dependent variables and using a task manipulation to create the effect of cognition. The two ads described by Buck et al. (1995, p. 446) were used as the stimuli in the experiments, and these two ads will be referred to as the patriotic and sexual ads in the study. The effect of gender, familiarity with the ad, and attitude to advertising on prosocial and reptilian feelings was also studied. In addition, I examined the effects of all these variables on attitude to the ad because this concept includes liking ratings that have been used in previous research on the independence of affect (Anand, Holbrook, & Stephens 1988; Zajonc & Moreland, 1977). The main research questions in the study were as follows:

1. Are prosocial and reptilian feelings evoked differently for (a) different types of ads and (b) the different types of task environments in which they are viewed?
2. Do certain types of ads evoke prosocial/reptilian feelings under certain task environments?
3. Are prosocial ads more effective in terms of attitude to the ad (liking for the ad)? Is this effect greater in a high task condition?

Hypotheses

As discussed, Buck et al. (1995) suggest that the sexual ad used in this study should evoke reptilian feelings of sex, power, and other feelings associated with the reptilian brain, as discussed by MacLean (1973, 1990). The patriotic ad, in contrast, should evoke prosocial feelings, associated with the centers of affiliation in the mammalian brain, such as compassion, sympathy, and sadness. Thus, there will be a main effect of each ad type, such that,

H1: Prosocial feelings will be higher in the patriotic ad than in the sexual ad.

H2: Reptilian feelings will be higher in the sexual ad than in the patriotic ad.

Kardes (1988) states that personal relevance (or involvement) should increase the amount of cognitive effort allocated to message processing. I submit that prosocial feelings are *not* independent of cognition and, in fact, require cognitive effort and, thus, will benefit from the cognitive processing present under conditions of high task involvement. Further, that this will be in evidence for the patriotic ad but not for the sexual ad in a high task/cognition condition. On the other hand, reptilian feelings *are* independent of cognition and, thus, they will benefit from a low task involvement condition in which there is less competition for processing capacity from cognition. This will be in evidence for the sexual ad but not for the patriotic ad under conditions of low task involvement.

Anand, Holbrook, and Stephens (1988) state that under the independence hypothesis, affect and cognition compete for processing capacity and that this resource competition view is completely opposite to the affect dependence hypothesis under which "an increase in cognitive processing should result in greater positive affect that should move cognition and affect together." Therefore, because cognition is more available for prosocial feelings in a high task involvement situation, prosocial feeling should be greater in the more conducive environment of the high task involvement condition, especially for an ad that promotes such prosocial feelings. Thus, prosocial feelings will not be higher simply because of the level of involvement (i.e., there will be no main effect of task involvement for prosocial feeling). It will depend on the nature of the ad as well.

H3: There will be an interaction effect of ad type and task involvement such that in a high task involvement situation, prosocial feelings will be higher than in a low task involvement situation for the patriotic ad.

If the resource competition view is correct and affect and cognition fight for processing resources (Anand, Holbrook, & Stephens, 1988), then reptilian feelings, which are independent of cognition, should benefit from a decrease in cognitive activity in the low task condition. Thus, reptilian feelings should be higher in the low task condition because there will be less competition from cognition in this condition. In the high task condition, reptilian affect and cognition will compete for processing resources and there will be less available resources in that condition so that affect generation will be hindered. As before, this will also depend on the type of ad (sexual in this case) and not on the level of task involvement alone. Obviously, subjects will not feel reptilian affect only as a function of the task involvement. However, the sexual ad in the low task condition should create greater reptilian affect than in the high task condition, and this difference should be greater than the difference in the two conditions as a result of the patriotic ad. Hence,

H4: There will be an interaction effect of ad type and task
involvement such that in a low task involvement situation
reptilian feelings will be higher than in a high task involvement
situation for the sexual ad.

Attitude to the ad measures usually include the like-dislike ratings
used in previous studies on the independence of affect. Thus, I included
attitude to the ad as a dependent variable in the study to see if the
results replicate any of the results for the prosocial or reptilian feelings.
It has been well documented that feeling responses influence attitude
to the ad (Brown & Stayman, 1992; Muehling & McCann, 1993). At the
same time, Stayman and Aaker (1988) found that not all the effects of
ad-induced feelings were mediated by attitude to the ad. Further,
Chaudhuri and Buck (1995) tested 240 ads for prosocial and reptilian
feelings and found that prosocial feelings were strongly and positively
related to liking for the ad (similar to attitude to the ad) but that
there was no relationship between reptilian affect and liking for the
ad. Perhaps reptilian affect is effective in other ways in advertising,
such as recall of the ad. Thus, because the patriotic ad should create
prosocial feelings and prosocial feelings have been related to liking,
I posit that

H5: Attitude to the ad will be higher for the patriotic ad than for the
sexual ad.

The Elaboration Likelihood Model (Petty & Cacioppo, 1986) posits
that attitude formation should be greater under conditions of high involvement. However, this holds for messages using central routes to persuasion
such as those found in rational, argument-based messages. The patriotic
and sexual stimuli in this study fall into the peripheral route category and,
thus, in keeping with the ELM, I posit that

H6: Attitude to the ad will be higher in the low task involvement
condition than in the high task involvement condition.

Because both ads are likely to follow the peripheral route, I do not
offer an interaction hypothesis for ad type and level of interaction with
attitude to ad as the dependent variable. In other words, there should
be no difference in attitude to the ad for the two ads based on the
level of task involvement. Also, the findings using like-dislike ratings in
past studies on the independence of affect (Anand, Holbrook, &
Stephens, 1988; Zajonc & Moreland, 1977) have provided conflicting
evidence. Thus, it is unwise to predict an interaction effect at this
juncture. At the same time, it will be interesting to note which, if any,
of the results of the other dependent variables may be reproduced for
attitude to the ad.

Method

Stimuli

Two print advertisements with no verbal elements were the stimuli in the study. These were chosen because previous research (Buck et al., 1995) identified these as effective in the elicitation of reptilian and prosocial feelings. It was expected that the "patriotic" ad with the soldier embracing the child would engender prosocial feelings whereas the other, "sexual," ad, depicting a half-naked man and a woman in a passionate embrace, would engender reptilian feelings. The ads were distributed to the subjects in a package containing the other elements in the study as described next.

Subjects and Procedure

One hundred and sixteen undergraduate students (67 men and 49 women) participated in a study with two different factors. In addition to the ad type factor, task involvement was manipulated in the following way. The high task involvement group was told that they would receive course credit for reading an article and correctly answering questions on the article. The article provided was a difficult piece on critical relativism and the falsity of realism, which required cognitive effort and concentration. Subjects were given a package containing the article on the first page, the ad (either patriotic or sexual) on the next page, and the questionnaire on the following pages. Before the article was handed out to the subjects, they were told not to turn to the second page until instructions to do so were given. Subjects were then given 5 minutes to read the first page. After that, subjects were asked to turn to the second page and look at the ad. Next, they were instructed to turn to the third page and fill in their ratings for the ad just viewed and to proceed on to the rest of the questionnaire. On completing the questionnaire, subjects were debriefed on the actual purpose of the study. In the low task involvement group, subjects were not told that they would receive course credit for the task or that they would have to answer questions on the article. The article provided in the low task group was a relatively light reading piece on English social history.

Manipulation Check

Three scaled responses at the end of the questionnaire served as checks on whether the high and low task manipulation was successful. A seven-point scale (anchored by "not at all" and "very much") was used for the following scale items: "How involved were you with the article? How much did you concentrate on the article? How much effort did you spend on the article?" For all three responses, the scores for the high task involvement group were higher and significantly different from the scores for the low task involvement group ($p < .01$).

Measures

The dependent variables were measured as follows on a seven-point rating scale. Subjects were asked to indicate how the picture they had just seen made them feel. Prosocial feelings were measured as the sum of subjects' responses to "sad, patriotic, sympathetic, compassionate, sorrowful, sentimental." Reptilian feelings were measured as the sum of the responses to "sexy, powerful, aggressive, excited, dominant, aroused." Principle components analysis of the 12 affect items showed two factors with eigenvalues greater than 1. The two factors explained 72% of the total variance in the items. All the prosocial items loaded greater than .76% on the first factor (39% of the total variance). All the reptilian items loaded greater than .77% on the second factor (33% of the total variance). Coefficient alpha for the prosocial items was .91. Coefficient alpha for the reptilian items was .92.

Attitude to the ad was measured as the sum of the responses to a seven-point semantic differential scale composed of "pleasant/unpleasant, favorable/unfavorable, likeable/unlikable, negative/positive, good/bad, interesting/uninteresting, irritating/not irritating." These items have been widely used to measure attitude to the ad in previous research (Muehling & McCann, 1993).

Controls

The following items served as two controls in the study. Prior familiarity with the picture was operationalized by "How familiar were you with the picture from before this task?" Attitude to advertising was measured as "In general, how much do you like advertising?" The means for these items (seven-point scale) were 2.18 and 5.02, respectively. Cox and Cox (1988) discuss how previous familiarity with an ad can affect attitudes, and MacKenzie and Lutz (1989) include attitude to advertising as an antecedent of attitude to the ad. Hence, these two items were included as co-variates in the study design.

Results

H1, H2, H3, and H5 were supported in the study, whereas H4 and H6 were not supported.

Prosocial Feelings as Dependent Variable

Analysis of variance for the effect of ad type on prosocial feelings found a significant main effect. Ratings for the patriotic ad (24.09) were significantly higher than for the sexual ad (10.25; $F = 114.55$; $p < .01$). Thus, H1 was supported.

As expected (H3), the effect of ad type was also moderated by a significant interaction effect of ad type with task involvement ($F = 10.51$; $p < .01$). The patriotic ad evoked greater prosocial feelings in the high task condition (25.88) than in the low task condition (21.71). The results were exactly opposite for the sexual ad in which greater prosocial feelings were found in the low task condition (12.81) than in the high task condition (8.15). This finding suggests that the patriotic ad benefited from the greater cognitive processing available to subjects in the high task condition and lends supports to the view that prosocial feelings are dependent on cognition.

No significant (p > .05) effects for gender differences, familiarity with the ads, and liking of advertising were found.

Reptilian Feelings as Dependent Variable

There was a main effect of ad type for reptilian feelings as well. Ratings for the sexual ad (16.47) were significantly higher than for the patriotic ad (10.77; F = 13.34; p < .01). Thus, H2 was supported. However, there was no support for H4 because there was no significant interaction between ad type and task involvement for reptilian feelings (F = .00; p > .10). Thus, reptilian feelings were in evidence (from H2), but these varied by ad type and not by the effect of task involvement on ad type.

Although not hypothesized, there was a marginally significant effect for involvement (F = 3.62; p < .10) and for gender (F = 3.46; p < .10). Reptilian feelings were greater in the low task condition (15.43) than in the high task condition (12.37). Also, reptilian feelings were higher for men (15.01) than for women (11.94).

No significant (p > .05) effects for the covariates, familiarity with the ads, and liking of advertising were found.

Attitude to the Ad as Dependent Variable

There was a significant main effect of ad type on attitude to ad. The patriotic ad was rated higher than the sexual ad (36.22 and 32.22; F = 6.86; p < .01). Thus, H5 was supported. However, there was no significant main effect for task involvement (F = 1.65; p > .10) and H6 was not supported. Further, there was no significant interaction between ad type and task involvement (F = .55; p > .10). Although nonsignificant, the scores across the four groups reflected the same pattern of scores as with prosocial feelings, that is, for the patriotic ad, the means were higher in the high task group (36.5) than in the low task group (35.88), and the pattern was reversed for the sexual ad in which the low task group was higher (35.11) than the high task group (29.85).

Interestingly, there was a significant interaction effect (F = 19.81; p < .01) of gender and ad type, such that women were lower than men in attitude to the ad scores for the sexual ad.

No effects (p > .05) for familiarity or liking of advertising were found.

Discussion

Prosocial and reptilian feelings were seen in this study to be different in nature and to be evoked under different conditions. Principal components analysis found two separate and orthogonal factors in the data on these feelings. Further, analysis of variance found that a patriotic ad evoked significantly greater prosocial feelings than reptilian feelings and that a sexual ad created significantly greater reptilian feelings than prosocial feelings. This is in keeping, generally, with previous research. Chaudhuri and Buck (1995) found that family appeals (based on affiliation, as are patriotic appeals) were positively related to prosocial feelings and negatively related to reptilian feelings. These authors also found that status appeals (based on power and dominance) were positively related to reptilian feelings but not related at all to prosocial feelings. Overall, there is evidence that these feelings exist independently and that they have different antecedents.

This study was also designed to see if these feelings occurred differently under different cognitive conditions. It was found that the patriotic ad created greater prosocial feelings under high cognition conditions than under low cognition. This finding confirms the cognitive-affective view of affect described by Anand, Holbrook, and Stephens (1988), which holds that if affect is dependent on cognition, it will be evoked more strongly under highly cognitive conditions. Interestingly, the sexual ad created fewer prosocial feelings in the high cognition condition than in the low condition. The sexual ad tended to inhibit and reduce prosocial feelings in a high cognition condition. For an ad that promotes reptilian feelings (as in the case of the sexual ad), which may be independent of cognition and not based on attachment to others, perhaps there was a "cognitive-affective crossfire" (Swann, Griffin, Predmore, & Gaines, 1987) or conflict in the high cognition condition such that prosocial feelings for the reptilian ad were lower in the high cognition condition than in the low task condition. In any case, the effect on prosocial feelings was exactly opposite for the two ads. Overall, consistent with expectations, there is evidence that certain types of affect (prosocial feelings in this study) are not independent of cognition.

However, contrary to expectations, the sexual ad did not generate significantly greater reptilian feelings than the patriotic ad in the low cognition condition over the high cognitive condition. Under the resource competition view described by Anand, Holbrook, and Stephens (1988), it was expected that the sexual ad would benefit from low cognitive conditions and elicit greater reptilian feelings under such conditions. Because reptilian feelings are not dependent on cognition, it was expected that a low cognition condition, where there would be less "competition" from cognition, would help the elicitation of reptilian feelings in contrast to a high cognition condition. Although the scores for both ads were higher in the low cognition condition, the interaction of ad type and task condition was not significant. Thus, based on the resource competition view, there is no evidence in this study that reptilian feelings are independent of cognition.

Future research needs to address two issues. First, is the resource competition view adequate in explaining feelings such as reptilian affects that may be independent of the processing mechanisms utilized for cognition? The resource competition view assumes that affect and cognition share a limited amount of processing capability. It is possible that reptilian feelings are not only independent of cognition, but also independent of the same processing facilities that produce cognition. If so, then the amount of reptilian affect will be completely independent of the level of cognition and reptilian feelings will be equally present regardless of the task condition. If reptilian feelings do not require cognition and do not share the same processing facilities, then the level of task involvement may not matter at all. According to MacLean (1990), the three brains have evolved literally on top of one another over the course of evolution, so it is possible that there are greater interconnections between the mammalian (prosocial, etc.) and neomammalian (cognition) brains than between the reptilian and the neomammalian. Perhaps future developments in brain research will shed more light on this aspect of reptilian feelings.

Second, we need to understand better the effects and consequences of reptilian feelings. The patriotic ad that produced greater prosocial feelings also produced better attitude to the ad scores than the sexual ad that was found to create greater reptilian feelings. Previous research also found that reptilian feelings were not associated with either liking for the ad or purchase intent for the brand (Chaudhuri & Buck 1995). How, then, do reptilian feelings influence advertising responses? The question would seem to be a critical one, given that we know that reptilian feelings exist and are qualitatively different from other feelings, and that a large amount of advertising appears to be sexual in its appeal. Status appeals, used in ads for cars and the like, are also "power" appeals that have been shown to produce reptilian feelings in previous research. Once again, it seems incumbent on consumer researchers to try to fathom the mysterious depths of these ancient emotional systems that are a part of the ancestral heritage of the human brain.

3

ATTITUDE FORMATION

O, reason not the need: Our basest beggars
Are in the poorest thing superfluous.
Allow not nature more than nature needs,
Man's life is cheap as beast's.

(King Lear, II, 4)

New luxury consumers are defined by their highly selective buying behavior.
They carefully and deliberately trade up to premium goods in specific
categories while paying less or "trading down" in many, or most,
others.... The criteria for their selective purchases are both rational –
involving technical and functional considerations – and emotional.

(Silverstein and Fiske, 2003, p. 23)

THE ROLE OF EMOTION AND REASON IN ATTITUDE FORMATION

Consumers develop attitudes about products, brands, and advertisements, and these attitudes influence their buying decisions. What is the role of emotion and reason in developing and forming such attitudes? And what are the implications for positioning brands in different types of product categories? This chapter tries to address some of these questions.

An attitude is an overall disposition towards an object or person. Allport (1935) spoke of attitudes as the single most important factor in social psychology. Subsequently, the attitude-behavior relationship has continuously been examined by researchers. Because consumer behavior does not correspond to a simple stimulus-response theory, marketers are today, more than ever, concerned about finding out how attitudes are formed and maintained. Are they the result of a logical, sequential, and propositional synthesis? Or are they emotional and intuitive? Does the consumer define specific, rational reasons for an attitude, or is this attitude a spontaneous liking for a product, unsupported by any intellectual motion towards this conclusion?

According to Fishbein and Ajzen (1975), a person's attitude consists of his salient beliefs. Beliefs are the subjective associations between any two distinguishable concepts ("I believe that Brand X is pure"). Such salient beliefs are activated from memory and considered in a given situation. This harks back to Rosenberg's (1956) multi-attribute definition of attitudes, in which attitudes are regarded as multidimensional and arrived at after evaluating several beliefs. Thus, by implication, such attitudes are more relevant for "high involvement" products, where evaluative criteria are more apparent and the degree of information processing on the brand's attributes is higher.

As seen in Figure 3.1, the traditional hierarchy of effects, as propounded by Lavidge and Steiner (1961), postulates that consumer attitudes are developed through a sequence of mental stages—cognitive, affective, and conative. Attitude formation on a brand thus starts with beliefs (the cognitive stage) about the brand. This learning process then leads to brand evaluation (the affective stage) or a total attitude towards the brand, which in turn leads to behavior change (the conative stage) in terms of action or, at least, as a tendency to act.

M. L. Ray (1973) subsequently demonstrated that the sequence of steps in the learning hierarchy, as described above, is not always the same. The cognitive aspect need not necessarily precede the affective, which must precede the conative. Attitude formation, Ray has shown, could well start with a conative or behavioral change (as in impulse purchases that may be preceded by very brief affects or rational cognitions). The consumer forms beliefs (positive or otherwise) about product attributes subsequent to purchase. Gorn (1982) and Mitchell and Olson (1981) also showed that the affective dimension could as well form the initial stage of attitude formation. The results of these experiments are discussed below and an alternative "hierarchy" is suggested with emotion as the initial catalyst in the process.

Gorn (1982) found that positive attitudes towards a product could develop as a result of the association of the product with music that had a positive effect on the listener. Hearing liked or disliked music directly affected product choice in his experiment. Gorn argued that the positive emotions generated by music become associated with the advertised product through classical conditioning. The liking for the ad gets conditioned onto the brand itself and becomes part of the brand. This can take place in

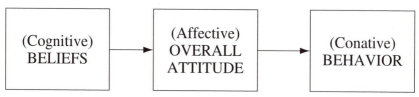

FIGURE 3.1   Three Components of Attitudes.

the total absence of cognitive beliefs. Product information was kept at a minimal level in the experiment. Mitchell and Olson (1981) also found that the same conditioning effect appeared to determine attitudes when nonverbal (visual) information, other than music, was presented. They exposed subjects to facial tissue ads that contained either a verbal claim or visual information. Individuals were seen to develop perceptions of brands based solely on visual, nonverbal information. They interpreted this as the classical conditioning effect of pairing an unknown brand with a visual stimulus.

It would appear, then, that consumers seem to be able to convert visual information into knowledge and beliefs about the attributes of the advertised brands. Thus, the advertisement produces a favorable emotional response in the consumer ("I like Brand X"), which brings about beliefs about the brand ("Brand X is healthy"), leading to a purchase intention ("I intend to buy Brand X"). This "alternative" hierarchy thus validates the use of "image" advertising in which the consumer "feels" the confidence of the product, rather than "reasons" it out. In today's world, major technological breakthroughs in terms of product attributes are few and more expensive to develop. Brand differences are difficult to find and promote for gaining a competitive edge. Consumers find it even more difficult to clearly experience these supposed differences. Emotional positioning offers new scope to product differentiation. Brands can now be positioned as "cool" or "fun" or just plain "happy," as in the case of a perfume by Clinique.

Thus, while product attributes are undoubtedly important for "high involvement" products, emotional communication is imperative for differentiating "low involvement" items and "parity" products, where actual product differences are either nonexistent or difficult to distinguish. It is clear today that even for high involvement products, the awareness stage of the product/brand life cycle need not be dominated by verbal information. Nonverbal, emotional advertising is viable throughout the product life cycle for almost all product categories and attains tremendous impact across all consumer segments due to its inherent ambiguity. We interpret such stimuli according to our personal needs and backgrounds—no one has to decipher the "correct" meaning for us and our interpretation is always true and accurate, so long as the stimulus produces a favorable response. Our "reasons" for liking it cannot be wrong. It is true because it is our own.

A MODEL OF EMOTION AND REASON IN BRAND ATTITUDE FORMATION

We have seen that the Fishbein model of attitude formation is largely formulated on a rational basis of multiple beliefs leading to attitudes and intention. Perugini and Bagozzi (2001), in their model of goal-directed behavior, have expanded the Fishbein model to include positive and negative emotions that lead to desire, which, in turn, provides the motivational element leading to intention to behave. I have taken their cue by including both emotion and reason in the formation of brand attitudes in the model depicted in Figure 3.2, which describes the effect of brand beliefs, brand evaluations, and brand attitudes on purchase intent and willingness to pay. Moreover, beliefs, evaluations, and attitudes have been broken down into their two components—rational and emotional. The model further specifies that tangible brand beliefs are more likely to be relevant for utilitarian goods whereas nontangible brand beliefs are more likely for hedonic goods (Holbrook & Hirschman, 1982). Hedonic goods are goods that provide enjoyment, pleasure, and fun (such as music CDs) to the consumer, whereas utilitarian goods (such as household cleaners) provide functional practicality (Okada, 2005). As Okada points out, hedonic and utilitarian goods are not on opposite ends of a continuum because it is quite possible for a good to be both hedonic and utilitarian (e.g., cars). Further, goods are neither hedonic nor utilitarian by nature. Any classification of goods as hedonic or utilitarian must rely on consumers' perceptions of their consumption of such goods as hedonic or utilitarian. Thus, hedonic and utilitarian goods in the model refer to consumer perceptions of goods and, accordingly, the units of analysis for all the constructs in the model are individual consumers. The model attempts to understand the place of product category perceptions, brand beliefs, brand evaluations, and brand attitudes in the brand intentions of individual consumers.

Rational or tangible brand beliefs ("this brand has fluoride") lead to rational brand evaluation ("this brand's benefits are worth the price") and utilitarian attitudes ("this is a good brand"), which in turn lead to purchase intent ("I intend to buy this brand"). On the other hand, nontangible brand beliefs ("this brand is fun") lead to emotional brand evaluation ("this brand is unlike other brands") and affective attitudes ("I love this brand"), which in turn lead to *both* purchase intent and willingness to pay ("I would pay a higher price for this brand over other similar brands"). Thus, these two routes to attitude formation and purchase intent are different because the emotional route also leads to willingness to pay whereas the rational route does not. This is important because purchase intent alone may not indicate a definite source of revenue for a brand for two reasons. First, because purchase intent may or may not translate into actual purchase and sales. Second, because revenue is a function of both sales and price and, hence, willingness to pay is also an important predictor of actual revenue. Ultimately, both emotional and rational routes are the best and most complete predictors of a brand's profit potential.

In Figure 3.2, I propose two different pathways resulting from two different types of brand beliefs into brand attitude formation. However, I do depict a path from tangible brand beliefs to emotional brand evaluation as

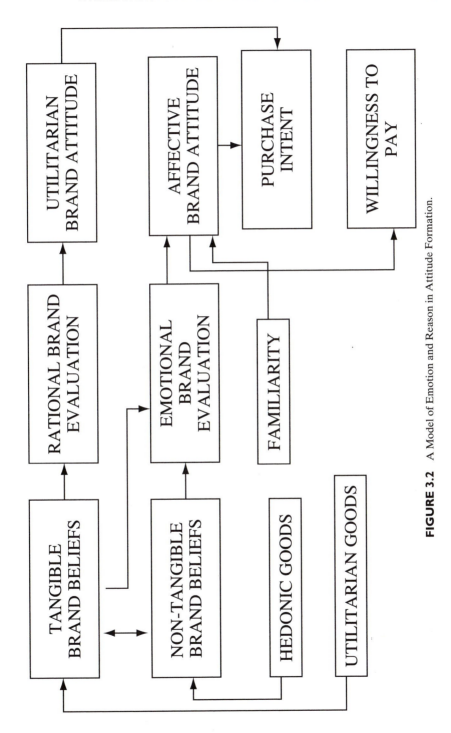

FIGURE 3.2   A Model of Emotion and Reason in Attitude Formation.

well because unique features in a brand should also lead to emotional brand evaluation ("this brand is unlike other brands"). Note that tangible and nontangible brand beliefs are also expected to correlate to each other; that is, a brand with tangible brand beliefs could also be associated with perceptions of nontangible brand beliefs, perhaps based on the advertising of the brand or based on some other set of benefits (friendly personnel, store environment, etc.). Note also that such brand beliefs are different from brand evaluations. Beliefs are descriptive facts based on the attributes of a stimulus whereas an evaluation involves a judgment on the structural relationships between the attributes. These descriptive beliefs belong to the objective attributes of the stimulus (such as price, features, reputation, etc.) whereas evaluative judgments are based on a subjective assessment of the structural relations between the attributes (such as "a good price" or "a fun brand"). Thus, a brand may be identified based on the ingredients it possesses, the packaging it has, its brand name, its price, and so on, but its evaluation of being a well-priced brand or a fun brand may be based on the relationship between the quality of the brand and its price, the nature of the advertising and its impact on the consumer's lifestyle, or the appropriateness of the brand's retail outlets. Both beliefs and evaluations are judgments, but one is descriptive, requiring less mental effort, and the other is evaluative and requires more mental effort. One is based on facts, the other on an analysis of the structure of these facts that make up the object. Including evaluations as an additional component in the attitude formation process allows us to better understand how beliefs become attitudes. An evaluation of existing beliefs leads to attitude formation.

My conceptualization of the two types of evaluations (rational and emotional) and their differential effects on utilitarian and affective attitudes is based on specific theories on the structure of evaluations by Mandler (1975, 1982) and others (Kohler, 1938; Perry, 1926). According to Mandler, we form evaluations on the basis of interactions between external events (brands in our case) and our existing schemas. A schema is a cognitive structure or abstract representation of reality that individuals use to guide thought and behavior, and it functions to provide an understanding of the environment. It is developed through repeated encounters with the environment and, in our case, it may be considered to represent the consumer's needs, personality, lifestyle, and all the facets that make up the individual consumer. The level of congruity between external evidence (say, a brand) and our existing schema (say, our needs) determines evaluations. Thus, any evaluation is a function of schema congruity or incongruity with an encountered stimulus. When a stimulus (brand) involves an existing schema and is congruous with the activated schema (needs), the result is a basic judgment of positive evaluation. Such an evaluation occurs when there is "... a reasonable fit between evidence and schema..." (Mandler, 1982, p. 20) and it may vary based on the type of stimulus and also on the situation or context (meets my needs for a toothpaste for my family) in which it occurs. Thus, it is a function of the individual, the stimulus, and the situation.

Such evaluations may combine with physiological arousal to create the subjective experience of affects such as anger, joy, and other qualitative affects. Thus, an affective attitude (say, "I love this brand") is constructed from an emotional evaluation and arousal, just as evaluations are themselves constructed from relations with the environment. Such arousal (and consequent affective attitude) only occurs when a stimulus is *in*congruous with existing schema. When stimuli are in congruity with schema, there is an absence of arousal and, thus, no subsequent affect and the result is a utilitarian attitude comprising basic liking ("this is a good brand") and acceptability of the stimulus as opposed to the affective intensity associated with the affective component of attitudes. Thus, basic liking or pleasantness of a stimulus is the result of rational evaluation and not an affect, which must be accompanied by arousal. Such a "constructionist" theory of emotion in which evaluations combine with arousal to produce affect (see also Schacter & Singer, 1962) would appear to be different from the theory of mere exposure (Moreland & Zajonc, 1977; Zajonc, 1980) in which emotion and reason are not necessarily considered to be part of the same process and may have separate mechanisms. The latter theory proposes that mere familiarity with a stimulus may lead to affect and, thus, I also include the effect of familiarity on affective attitudes in the model in Figure 3.2.

I submit that rational and emotional brand evaluations conform to the two types of evaluations (one arising out of schema congruity, the other out of schema incongruity) proposed by Mandler (1982). My definition of rational evaluation is conceptualized here according to the ideas of Mandler and others in cognitive psychology discussed throughout this chapter. Rational evaluation is defined as a positive evaluation of a brand based on the congruity between the tangible brand beliefs and the characteristics of the individual consumer. It is a basic, positive evaluation unaccompanied by arousal, whereas emotional evaluation is always accompanied by some level of arousal. This last type of evaluation can be either a positive or negative evaluation depending on the extent of incongruity of a stimulus on the schemas residing in the individual and the ability of the individual to assimilate or accommodate the stimulus into existing or new schemas. When the individual is not able to assimilate or accommodate the stimulus into his or her existing schemas, a negative emotional evaluation arises and gives way to negative affective attitudes such as "I hate this brand" or "this brand makes me angry."

Thus, I define emotional evaluation as a positive or negative evaluation of a brand based on the level of incongruity between the brand and other brands. As discussed, emotional evaluation results in at least some level of arousal based on the level of incongruity and the ability of the individual to assimilate or accommodate such incongruity. When the incongruity is slight, a process of assimilation results in a positive evaluation and a low level of arousal and affect. When the incongruity is high, a process of successful accommodation may lead to a positive or negative evaluation and higher levels of arousal and affective attitude. I do not model these processes of assimilation and accommodation here because Mandler clearly states that these processes are largely not conscious (see also the other references cited by Mandler, 1982 in this connection), whereas evaluations are conscious and lasting. Also, I model only the level of affective intensity (affective attitude in Figure 3.2) recalled by consumers from their past experiences with brands. I do not model actual physiological arousal because this is hard to measure; instead, I model the ability of consumers to self-report their affective states towards a brand in general and especially the affective attitude that the brand generates. I define affective attitude as consumers' self-reported level of the intensity of the subjective experience of positive feelings towards a brand in general and also in terms of their past brand experiences.

We have seen that Mandler asserts that events or objects that are in congruity with existing schema create evaluations involving positive liking (utilitarian attitudes in our case) that are not accompanied by arousal and, thus, are not evocative of affect. In discussing such simple evaluations, which involve basic acceptability of an object, Mandler (1982) states: "The kind of value that I have discussed is devoid of passion or fire. . . . Heat becomes an effective component of values once we move beyond mere schematic congruity" (p. 21).

Later, Mandler (1982) reiterates that schema congruity results in "0" intensity of affect (p. 22). Thus, I postulate that rational evaluation will not be related to the affective component of attitudes. Instead, I propose that rational evaluations will be directly related to the utilitarian component of attitudes because such basic positive evaluations are associated with a simple preference for the object of evaluation. An acceptable match between an individual's notions of price and quality, for example, and a brand's offerings on these same features result in a utilitarian interest (attitude) in the brand. I suggest that the outcome of rational brand evaluation is acceptability and a utilitarian interest in the brand, which I define as utilitarian attitude (see the next paragraph). Thus, I posit that rational evaluations will be positively related to the utilitarian component of brand attitudes but not to the affective component of attitudes.

Mandler and others associate evaluations of objects (say brands) with interest in that object. Perry (1926) also links interest to favorable attitudes towards the object. However, interest and evaluation are distinct concepts. Mandler argues that interest that is associated with evaluation is the result of interaction between the object and the person and that only certain things are of interest to certain persons. Because attitudes can also be associated with the interaction of certain consumer characteristics with certain product characteristics, I propose that brand attitudes are predispositions that can be regarded as a person's level of interest in a brand that results from the person's rational and emotional evaluations of the brand. Thus, attitudes are a function of both the brand and the person and they are based on a match between these two elements. Two aspects of attitudes, utilitarian and hedonic, have been well established in the marketing literature (Babin, Darden, & Griffin, 1994; Batra & Ahtola, 1991; Voss, Spangenberg, & Grohmann, 2003) and I use these in Figure 3.2 as two components of attitudes, utilitarian and affective. A utilitarian attitude is defined as a basic level of interest in a brand that is based on a rational predisposition for simple liking or acceptability of the brand and that leads to intent to buy the brand at a future date. An affective attitude is defined as a level of interest in a brand that is based on an emotional predisposition, positive or negative, towards the brand. Hedonic (affective) related criteria have been seen to relate to judgment (Adaval, 2001; Pham, Cohen, Pracejus, & Hughes, 2001; Yeung & Wyer, 2004).

Let us recap the most important points so far. Mandler associates occasions of schema incongruity (emotional brand evaluation, according to my definition) with rising levels of affective intensity, depending on the extent of incongruity and the ability of the individual to assimilate or accommodate such incongruity. An individual develops schemas about the tangible and nontangible benefits of brands based on interactions with various brands and uses these schemas to evaluate particular brands in terms of their fit. Emotional brand evaluation is the result of the incongruity, slight or severe, between a brand and the individual's schema, that has been assimilated into an existing schema (if slight) or accommodated successfully (if severe) into an alternate or new schematic representation. Such schema incongruity poses an "interruption," which temporarily or permanently blocks an individual's tendencies (Mandler, 1982, p. 14). Such an interruption, even slight, is sufficient to cause autonomic nervous system activity and, in turn, results in arousal and consequent affect. The extent of affect will depend on the extent of the disruption or interruption. Elsewhere in the literature on emotional and interpersonal communication we find a similar approach to the elicitation of affect. Berscheid (1983) delineates "love" as an interruption to an individual's planned activity. Hence, I posit that emotional brand evaluation leads to an affective attitude to the brand. (Other classic sources also document the relationship among arousal, interest, and incongruity. Berlyne [1960], for instance, suggests that discrepancies between events cause arousal, curiosity, and interest.) The relations between emotional brand evaluation and affective attitude will depend on the degree of arousal engendered by the interest, creating incongruity and, by the particular meaning, analysis that is engendered by the situation (p. 25). Thus, affective attitude should mediate the relationship of emotional brand evaluation with willingness to pay and purchase intent.

The two aspects of attitudes are expected to be associated with different types of antecedents and consequences. I model willingness to pay as a purely endogenous variable in the model and I define it as the propensity of a customer to pay a higher price for a brand despite the availability of similar brands at a lower price. The willingness to pay a higher price is the final outcome of an emotional process of brand evaluation. The process of this linkage between brand evaluation and a premium price is explained through the mediating influence of affective attitude in the model. Thus, a brand with unique qualities, tangible or nontangible, will be incongruent with existing schemas based on other brands, and will result in some level of arousal and affect. Positive affect will generate a level of interest or affective attitude to the brand. Affective attitudes, based on positive evaluation and positive affect, will foster a willingness to pay a premium price for the brand over other brands.

This is so because individuals who are interested in having an ongoing affective relationship with a brand may be willing to sacrifice resources to maintain such a valued relationship. Thus, they may be willing to pay a higher price for the brand over other similar brands. Accordingly, I suggest that when brand attitudes are affective and positive, they lead to a willingness to pay a higher price for the brand. The case for attitude strength leading to premium prices has been presented in earlier work (Keller, 1993). On the other hand, utilitarian attitude is a simple behavioral interest in the brand that results in an intent to purchase the brand. It is not necessarily indicative of a strong desire for the brand and, thus, is not capable of eliciting the sacrifice entailed in a willingness to pay a higher price for a brand over other similar brands. It is reasonable to expect that people will be willing to pay more for a unique brand with which they associate positive feelings.

MARKETING IMPLICATIONS

This has interesting implications for our understanding of market behavior by consumers. I have suggested that unique brands are more likely to be considered incongruous and thus elicit emotional brand evaluation leading to affective attitudes and a greater (than nonunique brands) willingness to pay a higher price for such a brand. This may help to explain why marketing textbooks often show that the demand curve (the relationship of price and quantity demanded) for prestige products may be upward sloping in direct contradiction with the laws of supply and demand in economics, which state unequivocally that as price goes down, quantity demanded increases. However, as suggested next, for certain types of products and certain types of consumers demand may actually go up as price increases.

Using an experimental manipulation in the form of a game between student subjects as buyers and computers as sellers, Amaldoss and Jain (2005) show that subjects who desire uniqueness (labeled as "snobs") are likely to increase their demand as the price of conspicuous products (prestige products such as cars, jewelry, watches, and perfumes) increases. In contrast, subjects who are "conformists" are likely to decrease their demand as price increases. Thus, snobs may want a higher priced product because they expect that at a high price there will be fewer people buying the product and this fulfills their craving for uniqueness. Thus, while on the aggregate (considering all buyers together) the demand curve for a product may indeed be downward sloping, if we disaggregate the marketplace into segments of consumers (see Hunt & Morgan, 1995 for a discussion), then it is very possible that certain segments (say "snobs") may display an upward sloping demand curve in their purchase behavior. Note that the behavior of snobs is not meant to signal their external status over others. This behavior is driven only by their internal need for uniqueness. Interestingly, and consistent with Figure 2.2, Amaldoss and Jain suggest that companies who make conspicuous goods emphasize the exclusivity of their products rather than the functional differences with other products in order to generate higher prices and higher profits.

RESEARCH RESULTS[1]

A Study of Emotion in AIDS and Condom Marketing

Background

India is the epicenter for the AIDS disease. Conservative estimates indicate that 10 million people in India will have been infected with the HIV virus by the year 2000 (Burns, 1996). It is a worldwide crisis of the gravest proportions, but nowhere is its potential more staggering than in India's population of more than a billion people who are at risk from an infection that is being spread from heterosexual activity.

The problem is exacerbated in India because, unlike in the United States, most AIDS cases arise out of heterosexual activity and the disease cannot be isolated to a few high risk groups like those using intravenous

---

[1] Parts of this research were published in Chaudhuri, Arjun & Ray Ipshita (2004). The effect of AIDS awareness on condom use intention among truck drivers in India: The role of beliefs, feelings and perceived vulnerability. *Journal of Marketing Communications*, *10*(1), 17–34.

drugs. In India, the disease is being spread by sexual contact between, for instance, male truck drivers and female sex workers (Burns, 1996). In spite of AIDS awareness campaigns that have already been broadcast on Indian television, the word on the street is that truck drivers will offer twice the amount to a sex worker *not* to use a condom. The consequences, however, may not be easy to shake as the truck drivers return to their villages, their wives, and their unborn children.

Purpose of the Study

The object of the study was to determine some of the antecedents of intention to use a condom among truck drivers in India. Does awareness of AIDS lead to condom intention or is this relationship mediated by rational beliefs about condoms and feelings about AIDS? Do individual-level variables like age, education, income, and frequency of sexual episodes have direct or indirect effects on condom intention? The answers to some of these questions may help the social workers and communication specialists who are currently fighting the pandemic in India. Personal intervention and message strategies in place today may, perhaps, be better targeted as a result of the findings of this study. The role of feelings, in particular, may play a pivotal part in such strategies in the future.

Research Expectations

The model used in this study attempted to examine the process by which AIDS awareness and individual characteristics lead to condom intention. Specifically, the model proposes that awareness of AIDS leads to perceptions of vulnerability to AIDS, beliefs about the benefits of condoms in preventing AIDS, and feelings about AIDS. These, in turn, lead to condom intention. Sociodemographic factors are also expected to influence perceptions and beliefs. Lastly, the model includes an individual level variable (number of sexual episodes) as an additional exogenous variable since it is likely that variance in this variable will be related to differences in perceptions, beliefs, and feelings about AIDS.

Research Methods

A study was conducted to test the model among 250 truck drivers in Calcutta, India. Interviews were conducted in six locations in the Greater Calcutta area using six interviewers and two supervisors for a total of 5 days. All the interviewers were males in their early twenties. A quota sampling method was employed according to an estimate of the total universe of trucks in these areas as provided by the field agency that conducted the interviews. An English questionnaire was translated into Hindi and Bengali versions because these languages are the most widely spoken in the Calcutta area. A "card" with a five-point scale (1 = not at all; 5 = a lot) was used for most of the questions. The card was made to resemble a petrol gauge, with which truck drivers are familiar.

Truck drivers in the sample area were all male and the average age was 35.36 years, ranging from 17 to 70 years; 79.6% were married and 89.2% had 0–9 years of schooling. Among the drivers, 63.9% spoke Hindi, 19.3% spoke Punjabi (but understood Hindi as well), and 12.4% spoke Bengali; 41.8% of the sample had at least one sexual encounter with a sex worker every month, ranging from 1 to 16 episodes per month.

Measurement

All measures were obtained from the information provided by the subjects in the questionnaire described above. Condom intention was measured as the sum of two five-point scale items ("If in the future you were to visit a prostitute, what are the chances that you would use a condom?", and "How much do you intend to use condoms in the future to guard against the AIDS disease?"). Perceived vulnerability was measured as the product of two five-point scale items—perceived severity of the threat ("To what extent do you think the AIDS disease is a threat to your life?") and perceived susceptibility to AIDS ("To what extent do you think that your occupation may expose you to AIDS?"). Feelings about AIDS were measured by the same five-point scale (1 = not at all; 5 = a lot). Subjects were asked to describe how they felt when they thought about the AIDS disease. Specifically, they were asked six separate questions: How sad do you feel? How afraid do you feel? How ashamed do you feel? How irritated do you feel? How lonely do you feel? How hopeless do you feel? Belief about condoms in AIDS was measured as the sum of two items that asked subjects for their level of agreement (same five-point scale as above) with two statements (a) "Using condoms during sex can help prevent AIDS," and (b) "Wearing a condom while having sex with a prostitute brings down the risk of AIDS." AIDS awareness was measured by two five-point scale items ("How much have you heard of the AIDS disease?" and "How much do you know about the AIDS disease?"). Because the two items had reliability (coefficient alpha) less than .50, they were not summed together but treated separately as single-item constructs in the analysis. Number of sexual episodes was measured by a single indicator—"On average, how many sexual encounters do you have with prostitutes every month?" The actual number of encounters reported was used as the measure for this variable. Age and income variables were also measured by the actual number of years and the amount in Indian rupees provided by the subjects towards the end of the interview. Education was treated as a continuous variable and measured by a six-point classification ranging from illiterate (no schooling at all) to college graduate.

Results

We can note the following significant results from the study:

- Hearing about AIDS is positively related to feelings about AIDS.
- Knowing about AIDS is negatively related to feelings about AIDS but positively related to beliefs about condoms in AIDS.
- Age is negatively related to condom intention.
- Beliefs about condoms in AIDS is positively related to condom intention.
- Feelings about AIDS is positively related to condom intention.
- Number of sexual episodes is positively related to perceived vulnerability.

See the final model in Figure 3.3 at the end of this chapter.

Conclusions

The results of the study appear to favor a mediated model of the effect of AIDS awareness on condom intention. Awareness of AIDS leads to beliefs and feelings about AIDS and these, in turn, lead to condom intention. Awareness does not directly lead to condom intention, but there is an indirect relationship routed through beliefs and feelings. Thus, beliefs and feelings about AIDS are intervening variables that help to explain why greater awareness of AIDS among truck drivers may lead to greater intention to use a condom during sexual encounters with sex workers.

On the surface, at least, the results imply that AIDS campaigns on television and in the media will be effective because greater awareness and beliefs and feelings about AIDS lead to greater intention to use condoms. However, the results also suggest that the real problem may still lie unaddressed. As expected, the number of sexual episodes was strongly and positively related to perceived vulnerability. However, perceived vulnerability was not significantly related to condom intention. Note also that although intention was nonsignificant ($t < 1.96$, $p > .05$), the simple correlation between these two constructs was significant and negative ($r = -.14$, $p < .05$). This is a terrible riddle. Why do people who see themselves as being greatly at risk not intend to use a condom on their next visit to a prostitute? One answer from the results of this study is that these people may also have low beliefs about benefits of condom usage in AIDS. Thus, AIDS and condom awareness campaigns may not be reaching the people with the highest risk of the disease—frequent users of prostitution.

Another possibility is that these "addicts" of prostitution knowingly opt for the pleasure of sex without a condom, in spite of knowledge about the consequences, just like heavy smokers, drinkers, and users of drugs continue to use products they know can kill them. If indeed these people are addicted to sex, then their treatment must match that of any other addiction. Mass media strategies promoting the use of condoms will not

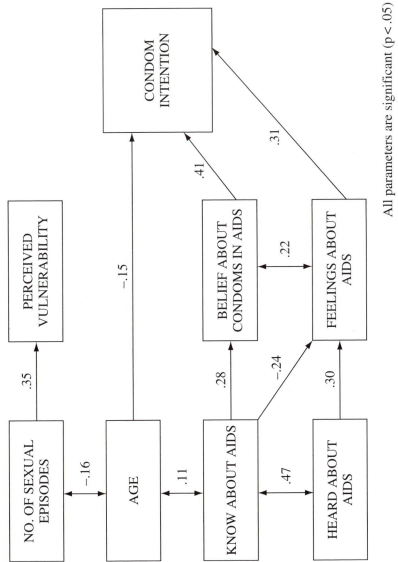

FIGURE 3.3 A Model of AIDS Awareness Effects.

All parameters are significant (p < .05)

work for heavy users of sex, just like they do not work for heavy users of cigarettes, drugs, and alcohol. Personal intervention methods, similar to those that are used for alcoholics, for instance, must be used to help them overcome their addiction. Some form of sexual rehabilitation may be needed for these people.

Summary

In summary, AIDS awareness campaigns have not always been successful in promoting greater condom usage. The results of this study indicate that awareness of AIDS will not directly affect condom intention. AIDS awareness must also result in beliefs about the efficacy of condoms in preventing AIDS and these beliefs, in turn, will lead to greater intention to use a condom. Additionally, increased negative feelings about AIDS (in conjunction with beliefs) were also seen in this study to be related to increased condom intention.

In terms of sociodemographic factors, only age was seen to be directly related to condom intention. Younger subjects reported more condom intention. Most interestingly, subjects with a higher frequency of sexual encounters with prostitutes were more likely to perceive themselves as vulnerable to AIDS, but their intent to use a condom during such encounters was not any greater than that of other subjects. In fact, there is some indication in the study that they may be less likely to develop condom intentions.

4[1]

INVOLVEMENT

Two kinds of love
One for the way you walk . . .
One for the way you love me . . .
(You're a great temptation)

(Stevie Nicks, Two Kinds of Love, 1989)

EMOTION, REASON, AND "INVOLVEMENT"

Research in marketing communication, advertising, and consumer behavior has been concerned with the concept of involvement. In general, there is agreement that the construct of involvement represents the notion of personal relevance or importance (Park & Young, 1986; Ratchford, 1987; Zaichkowsky, 1985). Further, Zaichkowsky (1986) has identified three different antecedents of involvement: person, object/stimulus, and situational factors. Zaichkowsky also describes three different domains of involvement: advertising, product, and purchase decision. However, it is not clear what the nature of involvement (or personal relevance) is in each of these domains. For example, it is uncertain what constitutes high personal relevance in the advertising domain. What mental outcomes, specifically, represent the involvement construct?

The subject of emotion and reason can be related to the literature on involvement and advertising and mass media research. For instance, the notion of two different styles of communication, discussed earlier, was anticipated by Marshall McLuhan (1964). According to McLuhan, television emphasizes more of the senses than print media. His statement, "the medium is the message" (1964, p. 7), seems to indicate that

---

[1] Parts of this chapter are reprinted with permission from 1992 AMA Educators' Conference Proceedings, published by the American Marketing Association, Chaudhuri, Arjun and Ross Buck, 1992, Vol. 3, 19–25.

ad content in television is not decoded in the usual rational information processing mode that may be applicable to media like print. McLuhan distinguished between "hot" and "cool" media. A "cool" medium, such as television, leaves more for the audience to fill in and, thus, elicits greater participation and involvement. Print media emphasizes the visual aspect of the senses, leading to a rational style of information processing that is logical and sequential. Electronic media, on the other hand, encourage a holistic style of processing that is emotional and involves all of the senses. In this sense, electronic media are more "involving" than print media. It is evident that McLuhan's ideas are akin to the concepts of spontaneous and symbolic communication discussed earlier. However, McLuhan did not specifically describe these two systems of communication as simultaneous and interactive.

Krugman (1965, 1971, 1977) also noted that television communicates very differently from the active, "working to learn" mode of communication used in print. In contrast to print, television transmits volumes of information effortlessly, and this information is capable of being retrieved at a later date when the same stimuli are recognized. Krugman defined involvement as the number of bridging connections that an ad makes with the viewer's personal life, and he viewed involvement as a function of left brain as opposed to right brain activity. Therefore, television ads are low in involvement because they make fewer connections and involve right brain activity.

Note that there is actually no role for emotion or affect in Krugman's theory—the consumer moves from awareness to purchase, with perhaps minimal beliefs after the purchase (Batra, 1986). Thus, a low involvement explanation of electronic media does not address situations in which the interaction of the systems of spontaneous and symbolic communication is especially relevant. In fact, until the late 1980s the marketing literature did not recognize that involvement may be composed of both emotional and rational responses. For instance, Ray and Batra (1983), who have contributed substantially to the topic of emotion in advertising, associated affective executions in ads with situations of low involvement in which there is low depth and quality of cognitive response. Park and Young (1986) were among the first to talk of "affective" involvement in advertising.

The Elaboration Likelihood Model postulated by Petty and Cacioppo (1986) describes two routes to attitude change and also associates affect with situations of low involvement. The personal relevance or level of involvement with the issue determines whether a message will be processed via the central or the peripheral route. If the level of involvement is high, it is more likely that the more thoughtful or central route to persuasion will be taken because the recipient is motivated to extend greater effort into the process. If the level of involvement is low, the peripheral route is taken and there is little or no consideration of the issue at hand. Instead, social cues and other factors irrelevant to the issue have an effect here, such as attractiveness of the source. Accordingly, the peripheral route results in simple inference as opposed to thoughtful assessment of the merits of an argument under the central route. Further, the peripheral route is seen to be less persistent in its effects and therefore less desirable as an outcome. In sum, the Elaboration Likelihood Model sidelines the role of emotion in persuasion, because it is viewed as an indirect route to attitude change that is less permanent and applicable only to situations of low involvement. Moreover, an "either/or" orientation is taken once again to the two streams of communication instead of recognizing that these may be parallel and simultaneous modes.

TWO TYPES OF INVOLVEMENT IN ADVERTISING

This book suggests that there are two different types of involvement outcomes. The first arises from spontaneous communication and results in knowledge by acquaintance (emotion); the second arises from symbolic communication and results in knowledge by description (reason). Involvement, in the advertising domain, can thus be viewed as the motivational potential of an advertisement, mediated by spontaneous and symbolic communication that activates both emotional readout and appraisal of this readout in terms of future goal-directed behavior. Accordingly, a low involvement advertisement would have to be one that is low in both emotion and reason and a high involvement advertisement is one that is high in either or both emotion and reason. This will be discussed further in this chapter and also when we examine the Advertising Differentiation Matrix in Chapter 5.

Buck and Chaudhuri (1994; see also Buck 1976, 1988; Buck, Anderson, Chaudhuri, & Ray, 2004) developed the ARI (Affect, Reason, Involvement) model, which is consistent with this definition of involvement. These authors define involvement as "the depth and quality of cognitive response" and include both affective (Emotion III) and rational responses as cognitions. Instead of thinking of affect and reason as two ends of a continuum, they conceptualize affect and reason as interactive components. Figure 4.1, based on Buck's (1976, 1988) developmental interactionist model, shows that the relative influence of affect and reason can vary, and this variance can be measured by an affect-to-reason ratio called the A/R ratio. Toward the left of Figure 4.1, affect is relatively more important than reason, while to the right the importance of reason predominates.

On the far left, for a sexual ad for example, the relative importance of affect can be close to 100% and that of reason almost 0. As we go further

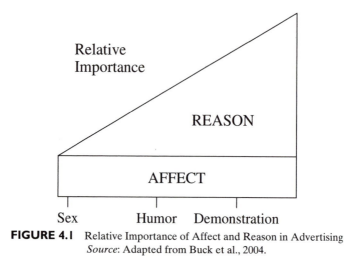

FIGURE 4.1   Relative Importance of Affect and Reason in Advertising
Source: Adapted from Buck et al., 2004.

to the right, the relative importance of reason goes up and reason becomes more important than affect. For a humorous ad, for instance, the proportion of affect and reason may be equal because humor is dependent on contrast, which has a rational basis. Further to the right, for an ad using a demonstration or comparison of product attributes, reason predominates over affect. However, the importance of affect never falls to zero, because there are no situations in which the role of emotion or affect is completely absent. In sum, we can think of a continuum not of affect and reason but of the relative values of these—the A/R continuum.

To illustrate, if affect and reason are measured on two 10-point scales, and affect has a score of 8 and reason has a score of 4, then the A/R ratio is 2. Note that a score of 2 and 1 on affect and reason, respectively, would produce the same ratio of 2. Thus, the absolute scores are not relevant when the relative score of affect to reason becomes the unit of measurement of the relative importance of affect and reason. In order to include the absolute scores as well, another measure can also be included. Buck and Chaudhuri (1994) consider involvement also to be the average of the scores of affect and reason. Thus, in the previous example, the involvement score would be 6 (8 plus 4 divided by 2). Accordingly, a low involvement advertisement, for instance, would be one with low scores on both affect and reason. An advertisement with a high score on either affect or reason would be a moderately high involvement advertisement, and an advertisement with high scores on both affect and reason would be a high involvement advertisement. Thus, the ARI model accounts for both absolute and relative measures of affect and reason and provides more complete information for managerial purposes. Note that both dimensions are indicative of involvement. As per the definition of involvement provided by Buck and Chaudhuri, one dimension accounts for the depth of response (the involvement score), and the other accounts for the quality of the response (the A/R ratio), both affective and rational.

PRODUCT INVOLVEMENT

The same framework can be used to understand product involvement. Figure 4.2 shows that consumers' choices of products can also be understood from the viewpoint of the relative importance of affect and reason. Candy, for instance, may be a purely affective purchase. Automobiles, however, may be purchased on both affective and rational bases, and appliances may have little affective appeal relative to reason.

Table 4.1 gives the affect mean, reason mean, A/R ratio, and involvement scores for 30 different product categories. As shown, although credit cards and autos both had a high involvement score, autos had a higher A/R ratio. The same is true for soft drinks and pharmaceuticals, snack foods and insurance. If you plot these scores on a graph like the one in Figure 4.3, you should get a dispersion of products across four types: products low on both involvement and A/R, products low on one but high on the other, and products high on both involvement and the A/R ratio. What implications would you draw for each of the four quadrants? I have taken the scores in Table 4.1 and assigned the products to four quadrants in Figure 4.3 on the following basis: Those products with A/R scores higher than 1 have been assigned to the high category and those with scores less than 1 to the low category; those products with involvement scores higher than 4 have been assigned to the high involvement category and the others to the low involvement category.

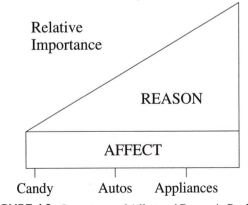

FIGURE 4.2 Importance of Affect and Reason in Products.

TABLE 4.1   Means and Ratios of Product Categories

Product	Affect Mean	Reason Mean	A/R Ratio	(R + A)/2
Autos	6.20	5.25	1.18	5.73
Candy	4.60	3.37	1.36	3.99
Sneakers	5.44	3.92	1.38	4.68
Appliances	2.78	4.71	0.59	3.75
Coffee	2.71	3.45	0.79	3.08
Cereal	4.60	3.20	1.44	3.90
Diamonds	5.40	4.62	1.17	5.01
Insurance	2.45	5.54	0.44	4.00
Beer	4.99	4.04	1.24	4.52
Dental hygiene	3.52	3.12	1.13	3.32
Soft drinks	4.81	2.92	1.65	3.87
Airlines	4.94	4.92	1.00	4.93
Long distance phone	3.83	4.57	0.84	4.20
House cleaners	2.23	3.14	0.71	2.69
Laundry products	2.59	3.35	0.77	2.97
Batteries	3.13	3.19	0.98	3.16
Wine	4.55	4.71	0.97	4.63
Paper products	2.47	2.73	0.90	2.60
Fast food	4.53	3.68	1.23	4.11
Snack foods	4.95	3.46	1.43	4.21
Credit cards	4.71	5.24	0.89	4.98
Camera film	4.73	3.89	1.22	4.31
Deodorants	3.12	3.20	0.98	3.16
Bath soap	3.28	2.78	1.18	3.03
Greeting cards	5.46	3.87	1.41	4.67
Pharmaceuticals	2.92	4.67	0.62	3.80
Personal computers	5.03	4.87	1.03	4.95
Express mail	3.24	4.06	0.80	3.65
Pet foods	2.35	3.27	0.70	2.81
Watches	5.16	4.12	1.25	4.64

There is a fair amount of dispersion of product types in the four quadrants in Figure 4.3. It appears that most products are either high on both involvement and A/R ratios or low on both. However, there are a fair number of products that are high on one dimension but low on the other. Thus, there are products, like cereal, that are not involving but

Involvement

	High	Low
A/R ratio — High	Products high in both involvement and A/R ratio scores (autos, sneakers, diamonds, beer, airlines, fast foods, snack foods, camera film, greeting cards, personal computers, watches)	Products low in involvement but high in A/R ratio scores (candy, cereal, dental hygiene, soft drinks, bath soap)
A/R ratio — Low	Products high in involvement but low in A/R ratio scores (wine, insurance, long distance phones, credit cards)	Products low in both involvement and A/R ratio scores (household cleaners, appliances, coffee, laundry products, batteries, paper products, deodorants, pet foods, pharmaceuticals, express mail)

FIGURE 4.3   Graph of A/R and Involvement Scores for Certain Products.

high in affective versus rational appeal. Conversely, there are products, like insurance, that are very involving but low in affective versus rational appeal.

INVOLVEMENT IN MASS MEDIA

A brand's position in the consumer's mind is also a function of the medium in which the brand is consistently promoted. How, then, do the various media function with regard to emotional and rational appeals? It is generally accepted in communication theory that mass media influence audience attitudes only indirectly via interpersonal sources such as opinion leaders (Klapper, 1960; Rogers, 1983). In situations of low involvement, however, mass media such as television are recognized to have direct effects on attitude formation through repetition (Krugman, 1965). This section presents the view that television also achieves direct effects on viewers through spontaneous emotional communication.

I suggested earlier that emotion and reason function differently with regard to two broad classes of media—broadcast (television, radio, etc.) and print (magazines, newspapers, etc.). It was suggested that print media generate a higher relative level of reason than broadcast media, whereas broadcast media elicit higher relative levels of emotional, affective response such as happiness and fear. In terms of affect and reason, we can once again depict a graph of the relative importance of these, and this time place print and electronic media with respect to their role in affective and rational responses.

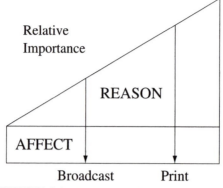

FIGURE 4.4   Two Types of Media Involvement.

As Figure 4.4 shows, and as suggested in the early part of this chapter, affect has higher relative importance for broadcast media and reason has higher relative importance for print media. This is also in accordance with the uses and gratification approach to mass media (Katz, Blumler, & Gurevitch, 1973) in which people are seen to use mass media to gratify different emotional and rational needs. Thus, in general, broadcast media may be used more for "diversion" and entertainment, while print media may be used more for "surveillance" and knowledge functions. Yet, one must be careful not to draw the distinction too tightly, because broadcast may be used for knowledge as well and print may be entertaining to some degree.

Gerbner and Gross (1976), in developing the "cultivation" theory of mass media, stress the same point. Although they claim that heavy viewers of television are more likely to express greater affect (fear about the real world), they also point out that for some people, television may be the only source of information. Because television is ubiquitous, free, and does not require literacy or mobility, it may be the only medium of information for "those who expose themselves to information only when it comes as entertainment. Entertainment is the most broadly effective educational fare in any culture" (p. 177). This notion of television as a great social leveler in the distribution of information through entertainment echoes Marshall McLuhan's ideas on the attainment of a "global village" achieved through the holistic impact of the electronic media. This has also been described earlier as the process of spontaneous emotional communication.

Buck (1989) argues that spontaneous cues are capable of being directly apprehended by viewers in the electronic media, just as the emotional displays (facial expressions, gestures, etc.) of persons are known directly by acquaintances in face-to-face communication. Moreover, this process of the transfer of affective meaning does not require the intervention of analytic, rational cognitions (no one has to explain the meaning of the displays). Zajonc (1980) also observed that a stimulus did not have to be consciously noted for it to influence emotion or behavior. Haley, Richardson, and Baldwin (1984) identified 510 nonverbal variables in television commercials in the areas of vocalics, proxemics, facial cues, music, and so on and related these successfully to persuasion variables such as brand salience. Some of these spontaneous cues, such as music, are available only in the broadcast media, and this is one reason for suggesting that, relative to print media, broadcast media provoke greater emotional responses. Buck cites evidence that with different musical renditions, liking of music videos is related to markedly different feelings of happiness, sadness, fear, and anger. Chaudhuri and Watt (1995) also found that music is significantly related to happiness responses in radio commercials.

On the other hand, Park and Young (1986) found that music in television commercials had a distracting effect during analytic cognitive situations. The lack of such cues as music in print media may thus encourage analytic cognitive responses, at least in comparison to broadcast media. Further, according to Batra (1986), consumers are more active and willing to process information in print than in broadcast, which is considered to be more "intrusive." In keeping with this, Jacoby and Hoyer (1990) found less miscomprehension for print ads than for television ads. Wright (1974) showed that print media mediate analytic cognitive responses to advertising, such as source derogation and counterarguing. He suggested that this is because print allows more opportunity to process information, because it is spatial, whereas electronic media are fleeting and not in the control of the viewer. Although Wright did not examine syncretic cognitions, another study by Chaudhuri and Buck (1990) found significant differences in the effects of television, radio, and magazines across 11 of 14 affective responses, such as happiness. Significant differences in the three media formats were also noted for reactions to the cognitive content of the advertisements, the likeability of the advertisements, and the intention to buy as a result of the advertisements.

Media research on left and right brain hemispheres also shows different effects for broadcast and print media. Weinstein, Appel, and Weinstein (1980) found that print generates more left brain activity than television. Krugman (1971) showed that the nature of brain wave activity was very different for print as compared to television, and he attributed this to the fact that we act on print, whereas television acts on us. I further suggest that, in general, spontaneous communication via broadcast media results in emotional right brain activity, while symbolic communication through print media results in rational left brain activity. There is considerable evidence that left and right hemispheres are associated with reason and emotion, respectively. Thus, in general, an advertisement in print media requiring linguistic-analytic processing particularly involves the left hemi-sphere, whereas an advertisement in broadcast media requiring a direct form of empathy with emotional expression and an integration of sensory information particularly involves the right hemisphere. The caveat must be provided that we are discussing the relative importance of the systems of emotion and reason. Left and right brain hemispheres also balance, modify, and interact with each other.

In sum, electronic media, such as television, are a form of communication that is inherently different from print, and not simply because of the additional advantage of the auditory channel. It is the dynamic combination of movement, color, sound, video, iteration, drama, and general emotional impact, expressed through spontaneous nonverbal cues, that makes television such an effective purveyor of emotional communication.

RESEARCH RESULTS[2]

A Study of Hedonic and Analytic Values in Products

Purpose of the Study

This study attempted to develop a typology of product categories, based on the hedonistic and analytic criteria used by consumers. It is entirely plausi-ble that a product can be capable of simultaneously eliciting *both* emotional and rational responses. Thus, the present study attempted to classify a large number of product categories on separate hedonic and analytic dimensions.

Theoretical Background

On the level of product categories, we can conceive of two types of con-sumer knowledge—one that is acquired by direct sensory experience with the product and another that is ratiocinative and involves analysis and judgment. The first is the *hedonic* value of a product, which is known directly through immediate and subjective experience with the product and that results in a sensation of *pleasure*; the second is the *analytic* value of the product, which can be described in terms of judgments concerning the functional attributes of the product. Consumers today are faced with many competing versions of the same product, so these judgments are fur-ther seen to relate to the *perceived differences* between brands.

---

[2] This research is reprinted with permission from the Association of Consumer Research and originally appeared as Chaudhuri, Arjun. 1993. Advertising implications of the pleasure principle in the classification of products. In W. Fred van Raaij and Gary J. Bamossy (Eds.), *European Advances in Consumer Research* (Vol. 1, pp. 154–159). Provo, UT: Association for Consumer Research.

Thus, certain products are viewed as pleasurable, irrespective of the brand that is purchased. In general, this would apply to parity products, such as beer, chocolate, liquor, sodas, and the like, where brand differences are imperceptible to most consumers but where the pleasure component is high. On the other hand, certain products are viewed as risky, in the sense that consumers realize that significant differences exist between brands and that the wrong brand could bring about deleterious consequences. Murphy and Enis (1986) identified five such consequences of risk—financial, social, psychological, physical, and functional. Such perceived risk is a function of perceived quality differences between brands (Bettman, 1973) and leads to active information search and evaluation. Moreover, our understanding of advertising strategy and its effects is significantly richer when you consider that for certain product classes consumers may process information in *both* highly analytic and hedonistic ways and that for other categories evaluation may be low in both as well.

Measurement

The choice of *pleasure* and *perceived differences* as operationalizations of the two substantive dimensions of involvement in the classification of products, with special regard to advertising, is well vindicated by past research. Preston (1970), demonstrated that perceived differences in the products advertised in magazines and television could account for high and low involvement effects. Robertson (1976) viewed "commitment" to be a function of "perceived distinguishing attributes among brands and the salience of these attributes" (p. 23). Bowen and Chaffee (1974) considered involvement with a product to increase with the "number of pertinent distinctions" (p. 165) between brands. Zaichkowsky (1985) also found a positive relation between perceived differences between brands and the level of involvement.

In presenting an alternative to the usual information-based perspective on consumer behavior, Holbrook and Hirschman (1982) advocated research on the experiential aspect of human consumption in which emotions and feelings of enjoyment and pleasure are the outcomes. Laurent and Kapferer (1985) found that the hedonic value of a product had a significant effect on communication variables such as exposure to advertising. In the same study, perceived differentiation was seen to be related to the extensiveness of the decision process, which was treated as a consequence of involvement. However, pleasure value was *not* related to the extensiveness of the decision process, thereby suggesting that pleasure and perceived differentiation have different effects and represent orthogonal dimensions. In another study, Zaichkowsky (1987) found support for the FCB (Foote, Cone and Belding) grid using a measure emotion (exciting/ unexciting) similar to pleasure.

Havlena and Holbrook (1986) documented that dimensional aspects of emotion (Mehrabian & Russell, 1974) such as pleasure provide greater information about consumption experiences than do typological (Ekman & Friesen, 1975) aspects of emotion, such as happiness and fear. In general, the role of pleasure has increasingly been heralded by researchers, and a basic premise in this study is that human beings have always been motivated by the pursuit of pleasure and the avoidance of pain.

The Study

Two scales were used to operationalize the concepts of hedonic and analytic value:

> "How likely is it that these products could give pleasure to most people?"
> "How much difference can most people perceive in the quality of brands of the following?"

Single-item scales that provided clear face validity for the theoretical constructs, as defined earlier, were necessary in order to obtain ratings on a large number of categories from the same individuals. The intention was to determine whether a more parsimonious method, using different operationalizations, could still reproduce the findings of the FCB grid in which product classes were found to be dispersed over four mutually exclusive quadrants.

Both scales were intentionally constructed to be read in the third person; otherwise, product usage might bias responses. Also, the use of "most people" is a projective technique that allows an indirect approach to issues that might otherwise be repressed (Havlena & Holbrook, 1986).

Seventy-six product classes were rated on each of the two scales by 216 undergraduate students at a Connecticut university. All product classes were first rated on one scale, and then the second scale was introduced for the same product classes. Questionnaires were pretested and counterbalanced to guard against order and fatigue effects. The list of product classes was generated from a variety of sources, which included an exploratory study of commonly used products. Table 4.2 provides the means for each product class computed for both the hedonic and analytic scales. Seventy-two of the 76 pairs of means revealed a significant correlation (person product moment) between hedonic and analytic values at the .05 level.

Figure 4.5 shows a graph that plots these mean values for each product class. A clear one-dimensional trend can be seen in these values in the figure. The correlation coefficient between the means of analytic and hedonic value was computed as .72. This is in accordance with the expectation that relevant aspects of involvement are likely to correlate positively together (Laurent & Kapferer, 1985). It can be concluded that products that are rated high on hedonic value are also rated high on analytic value. Similarly, products rated low on hedonic value are rated low on analytic value.

TABLE 4.2 Hedonic and Analytic Means of Products

	Hedonic Mean	Analytic Mean		Hedonic Mean	Analytic Mean
Vanilla ice cream	4.847	4.023	Washing machines	3.889	4.094
Running shoes	4.150	5.283	Cottage cheese	3.200	3.294
Light beer	4.648	4.493	Telephone service	4.886	5.592
Perfumes	4.268	4.058	Window cleaners	3.399	2.986
Regular instant coffee	3.654	3.720	Color TVs	5.870	5.360
Health insurance	4.412	4.897	Laundry detergent	3.358	3.780
Chocolate bars	5.028	4.425	Airline service	4.505	4.921
Suitcases	3.353	3.399	Gasoline	3.542	3.140
Cigarettes	3.620	4.399	Baseball gloves	3.744	3.860
Mortgages	2.526	4.551	Roll-on deodorants	3.394	3.808
Chocolate chip cookies	5.262	4.659	Luxury cars	6.065	6.230
Photocopiers	3.893	4.164	Pantyhose	3.500	3.794
Frozen yogurt	4.200	3.763	Personal computers	4.786	5.437
Microwave ovens	5.056	4.804	White bread	3.805	3.594
Swimwear	4.718	4.647	Life insurance	4.514	4.972
Floor polish	2.532	2.874	Unrecorded videotape	3.468	3.428
Nail polish	3.214	3.274	Savings accounts	5.293	4.474
Fabric softener sheets	3.340	3.084	Tennis rackets	4.144	4.607
Pretzels	4.023	3.195	Canned chicken soup	3.563	3.374
Bubble gum	4.250	3.746	Sports cars	6.167	6.260
Gel toothpaste	3.767	3.396	Wine coolers	4.958	4.572
Designer jeans	4.332	4.721	Camera film	4.154	3.953
Vacuum cleaners	3.394	4.088	Dishwashing liquids	3.144	3.140
Compact cars	4.425	5.423	Diet colas	4.131	4.089
Typewriters	3.654	4.382	White boxer shorts	3.409	2.514
35 mm cameras	4.894	5.493	Lipstick	3.556	3.625
Bath soap	4.381	3.824	Frozen orange juice	3.891	3.688
Compact disc players	5.605	5.477	Ketchup	3.735	3.514
Home furniture	5.037	5.162	Facial tissues	3.745	3.584
Chocolate cake	5.094	4.245	Envelopes	3.307	1.963
Facsimile machines	3.577	3.995	Regular potato chips	4.135	3.931
Ballpoint pens	3.696	3.251	Paper towels	3.468	3.391
Low calorie mints	3.609	2.698	Writing paper	3.554	2.417
Backpacks	3.460	3.394	Light bulbs	4.130	2.679
Toilet tissue	4.386	3.968	Peppermint schnapps	4.556	3.507
Skis	4.387	5.285	Mustard	3.381	3.330
Cotton socks	4.243	3.257	Chewing tobacco	2.736	3.557
Pick-up trucks	4.033	5.402	Diapers	2.907	3.856

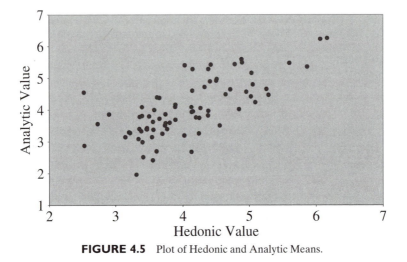

FIGURE 4.5   Plot of Hedonic and Analytic Means.

In order to test this conclusion further, a principal components factor analysis was conducted using the mean scores for each product class on hedonic and analytic value. As expected, a single factor was extracted that explained 86% of the variance in the variables. Thus, although the two dimensions or the matrix appear to be present, it must also be noted that there may be a higher order, superordinate construct that determines consumer perceptions of hedonic and analytic value. It is suggested that this is quite possibly the concept of "involvement." Consumers who are involved with a product class tend to view it as both pleasurable and capable of brand differentiation. Conversely, consumers who are not involved with a product class tend to view it as incapable of both brand differentiation and pleasure gratification.

There are exceptions to this, as in the case of mortgages, for example, but by and large consumers seem to perceive that both aspects vary together. A clear one-dimensional trend was observed in the study, and it is suggested that this may be due to the higher order construct of involvement.

Discussion

Of course, the results may be due to the limitations in the study. For instance, there are limits on generalizability, because the undergraduate subjects used in the study may be expected to possess higher levels of interest for certain products such as beer and lower interest for products such as diapers. Future research must be conducted among more representative samples, so that demographic differences do not confound the findings. Further, one cannot be sure that the two measures used in the study are truly indicative of the involvement construct. Future research must determine the relationship of these measures to an independent measure of involvement, such as Zaichkowsky's involvement scale (1985), and also to involvement outcomes such as quantity of information search, in order to establish the validity of these measures in terms of the involvement construct.

In spite of these limitations and on the basis of what is only an exploratory study, one can, perhaps, still speculate that the one-dimensional trend observed in the study can be attributed to the pleasure–pain paradigm. Perhaps both measures in the study are assessing a fundamental and overriding principle in human behavior—the search for pleasure and the avoidance of pain. For instance, in the case of luxury cars, which are high in pleasure value, there is also the possibility of extreme pain due to the existence of high brand differences in the analytic value of the product.

Accordingly, in terms of product involvement, a stimulus that has sufficient motivational potential (i.e., *pleasure*) leads to appraisal of the product category in terms of brand differences and other analytic functions. The capacity for pleasure in the stimulus generates cognition (knowledge by acquaintance) and, if sufficiently pleasurable, leads to cognitions that understand and describe the stimulus—product. Left and right hemispheres in the human brain work *together* and are not at odds with each other. Thus, high involvement products are high in *both* hedonic and analytic aspects, and low involvement products are low in *both* as well. Financial risk and the like is endured *only* if the product has the potential for pleasure. Of course, this pleasure can take many forms: intellectual (books), sensory (foot massagers), status (clothing, etc.), problem solving (computers), and even freedom from pain (pharmaceuticals).

The implications for advertisers are clear. For high involvement (i.e., pleasurable) products, ads should show both the pleasure that can be derived from the product *and* the functional differences between brands in the product category. For low involvement products, ads should produce ad-induced pleasure from the presentational elements in the ad, because such products lack the inherent motivational potential to produce pleasure. In either case, pleasure is always relevant. Advertisers are already cognizant of the pleasure–pain motive, because ads today, for certain types of products, produce their effect by depicting pain (through fear appeals, for instance) and *then* providing relief from the pain, achieved through the use of the advertised brand.

5[1]

THEORIES OF LEARNING

Emotions bind us to the past in mysterious ways. Sometimes these feelings are awakened quite suddenly. Walking as a grown man through a Hawaiian forest I inhaled the sweet, sickly smell of the frangipani flower that grows in the tropics. It was an odor redolent of memories dormant for years. My senses reeled from the forgotten pleasure of the rich, lush smell and I hurtled back into the picture palaces of the past. Memories of soccer on the streets, of tobacco-coated old uncles long gone, of childhood scrapes and scraps. Memories of the quiet of the afternoon heat and the click of the garden gate as someone left the house. Memories of tea and laughter in our garden under the tree from which the frangipani fell. And the silence of the house when someone died and the fragile white flowers lay crushed under our feet.

(Anonymous)

A men's cologne manufacturer recently sprayed young men on spring break in Florida with a free sample of cologne. They expected that the smell would become associated with pleasant memories of spring break and that this would result in sales later in life when the same fragrance was sampled again in a store and happy memories resurfaced. Federal bodies and corporations are also testing the influence of smell in producing greater employee output. Is there a smell that can trigger greater aggression among troops? Is there a whiff that can make workers more energetic?

This is one example of the classical conditioning theory of how emotions gain their effect. This and other theories of how learning takes place through emotion and reason are the subject of this chapter. I will also depict the best choice of media strategies when using each of these learning strategies. Learning theories are particularly important in understanding

---

[1] Parts of this chapter are reprinted with permission from 1992 AMA Educators' Conference Proceedings, published by the American Marketing Association, Chaudhuri, Arjun, 1992, Vol. 3, 442–446. Parts of this chapter were also published in Chaudhuri, Arjun & Ross Buck. 1997. Communication, cognition and involvement: A theoretical framework for advertising. *Journal of Marketing Communications*, 3(2), 113–125.

advertising effects because consumers learn about brands and products through advertising and other promotional strategies used in marketing. How this learning actually takes place and which medium is best suited for each learning outcome is the subject of this chapter. Knowing the process means that we can influence it and help it towards fruition. In this chapter I also introduce the useful concept of the Advertising Differentiation Matrix, which incorporates five of the learning theories, and I contrast it to the well-known FCB (Foote, Cone and Belding) grid (Vaughn, 1980). Finally, I provide some empirical evidence for the matrix in the Research Results section.

In all, three broad classes of theories of advertising strategy have been identified: systematic, heuristic, and affective (Pechmann & Stewart, 1989). Affective theories can be further divided into theories of classical conditioning, vicarious learning, and product-induced affect. These five theories of advertising strategy will be discussed in this chapter, and their relationship to emotion/affect and reason/cognition will be examined.

SYSTEMATIC LEARNING THEORIES

Systematic learning theories, based on the traditional information processing paradigm in consumer behavior (Bettman, 1979), view the consumer as an active processor of information. The recipient of a persuasive message goes through the process of attention, comprehension of the message, rehearsal of the message (which produces a suitable conclusion), and finally, retention of the message in memory. Thus, it is the verbal content of the message, or symbolic communication as described in chapter 1, that is the primary determinant of beliefs and judgments about brands under conditions of systematic learning. This process of the creation of beliefs and judgments about brands on the basis of symbolic advertising communication is also the process of developing knowledge by description, which is based upon reason.

Thus, the generation of reason is linked to the systematic learning of product and brand information from ads. Such systematic learning is also likely to generate greater rational responses when it is used in the print media, because print allows greater opportunity to process verbal information about brands. Wright (1974) showed that print media mediate rational responses to advertising, such as source derogation and counterarguing. He suggested that this is because print allows more opportunity to process information, whereas electronic media are fleeting and not in the control of the viewer. Further, according to Batra (1986), consumers are more active and willing to process information in print than in electronic media, which are considered to be more "intrusive." In keeping with this, Jacoby and Hoyer (1990) found better comprehension for print ads than for television ads.

Systematic learning processes that generate reason may also be understood in terms of left hemisphere brain activity, and media research has shown different hemispheric effects for electronic and print media. Weinstein, Appel, and Weinstein (1980) found that print generates more left brain activity than television. Krugman (1971) also showed that the nature of brain wave activity was very different for print as compared to television, and he attributed this to the fact that we act on print, whereas television acts on us. Additionally, Tucker (1981) and Buck (1988) cite considerable evidence that left and right hemispheres are associated with the two different kinds of cognition (analytic and syncretic) discussed earlier. Thus, it is suggested that an advertisement in print media requiring linguistic-analytic processing particularly involves the left hemisphere and systematic learning processes, whereas an advertisement in electronic media that encourages a direct response to emotional expression and an integration of sensory information particularly involves the right hemisphere. The latter type of expression involves spontaneous communication, as described in chapter 1, and may also be understood in terms of the three learning theories described next.

HEURISTIC LEARNING THEORY

According to Chaiken (1980), people process information in both systematic and heuristic ways. Whereas systematic processing involves thoughtful, "mindful" analysis of the content of the ad, heuristic processing involves the use of simple heuristic cues in order to arrive at a conclusion (brand preferences, etc.). Thus, consumers may sometimes use simple decision rules (or "rules of thumb") in their behavior, such as buying a brand name, buying the brand advertised by an expert, attractive, or trustworthy spokesperson; buying the brand that most people use; or buying the brand that is advertised the most.

Pechmann and Stewart (1989) argue that heuristic processing is the antithesis of analytic processing, because this process is used when consumers wish to *avoid* detailed consideration of the merits of a brand. The implication may then be made that heuristic consumers wish to expend less effort in decision making. Relatedly, Krugman (1965) has argued that television functions as a low involvement medium that uses heuristic cues (repetition of the brand name, etc.) for its effectiveness. Chaiken and Eagly (1983) also associate heuristic processing with electronic media and systematic processing with print media, because print media is better used for presenting difficult messages whereas electronic media, because it is fleeting, is better for simpler heuristic messages.

Petty and Cacioppo (1986) have also suggested two routes to persuasion: a central, more thoughtful route under conditions of high motivation and a peripheral (heuristic/affective) route to persuasion when motivation to think about a message is low. In contrast to the central route, the peripheral route entails little or no consideration of the issue at hand. Instead, social cues and other affective factors irrelevant to the issue have an effect here, such as the attractiveness and likeability of the source.

Thus, affective cues, such as a celebrity spokesperson, may generate emotion and elicit heuristic processing. Accordingly, heuristic processing may be associated with greater emotional responses. In other words, under conditions of low involvement, people may use the affective response to an ad as a heuristic to decide which brand to buy ("I *like* the *advertising* for this brand, therefore, I will choose this brand"). Ray and Batra (1983) state that emotion-laden stimuli in ads may create better message acceptance, because in a positive affective state, people tend to make speedier, less complex judgments. The use of visual, sensory, nonverbal imagery may discourage counterargument and reason and facilitate persuasion via affective cues that generate emotion. Further, such communication is also more apt to take place on television, due to its capacity for greater vividness of the images presented, as described by Chaiken and Eagly (1983).

CLASSICAL CONDITIONING

In their now-classic experiments, Pavlov (1927) and others (Watson & Rayner, 1920) demonstrated that if two dissimilar objects are repetitively associated together in close contiguity to each other, the emotional response originally elicited by the unconditioned stimulus can, over time, be elicited by the conditioned stimulus alone. Mitchell and Olson (1981) also found that the same conditioning effect appears to determine attitudes when *nonverbal* information is presented in advertisements. They exposed subjects to facial tissue ads that contained either a verbal claim or nonverbal information. Individuals were seen to develop perceptions of brands based solely on nonverbal information. Mitchell and Olson interpreted this as the classical conditioning effect of pairing an unknown brand with a nonverbal stimulus.

Thus, over time, advertisements that associate a brand with a nonverbal affective cue transfer the affect to the brand itself. This involves spontaneous communication, which transfers the affect associated with the nonverbal stimulus in the advertisement to the brand's image. It is different from symbolic communication in that it is not a linguistic process and there are no formal rules involved. Moreover, electronic media may be especially adept at classical conditioning strategies that produce emotion, because electronic media abound in spontaneous, nonverbal emotional cues. Indeed, Haley, Richardson, and Baldwin (1984) identified 510 non-verbal variables in television commercials in the areas of vocalics, proxemics, facial cues, music, and so on, and related these successfully to persuasion variables such as brand salience.

The importance of nonverbal elements, such as music, in evoking affective response is also well documented (see Haley et al., 1984). For instance, Gorn (1982) found that positive attitudes towards a product could develop as a result of the association of the product with music that had a positive effect on the listener. Hearing liked or disliked music directly affected product choice in his experiment. Gorn argued that the positive emotions generated by music become associated with the advertised product through classical conditioning. The liking for the ad gets conditioned to the brand itself and becomes part of the brand. This can take place in the total absence of reason or beliefs, because product information was kept at a minimal level in the experiment.

In sum, classical conditioning strategies in advertising commonly use spontaneous nonverbal cues, such as music, which generate emotion. Some of these spontaneous nonverbal cues, such as music and sound effects, are available only in the electronic media and, accordingly, I suggest this as a second reason why, relative to print media, electronic media emphasize emotion. Moreover, it has been found that music in television commercials has a distracting effect during rational situations (Park & Young, 1986). The lack of such cues as music in print media may thus encourage rational response, at least in comparison to electronic media.

VICARIOUS LEARNING

Pechmann and Stewart (1989) describe the process of vicarious learning through advertising. Ads that portray reward or punishment for an actor due to use or nonuse of a particular brand arouse identification and emotion. The point is that humans construct beliefs—rules about which brands/products to use—based on emotional communication. The rewards/punishments meted out to the model in the ad are exemplified in the model's expressive behavior, such as facial expressions; the process of observing such emotional expressions results in arousal and a vicarious sharing of the same subjective experience as undergone by the model in the ad. The consumer comes to associate the brand with the emotion generated (happiness, say) and sees the brand as the social instrument that obtains rewards and stays punishments.

Buck (1989) argues that spontaneous emotional communication via electronic media is responsible in part for the "emotional education" of persons in that it provides an understanding of the internal environment of feelings and desires. Such communication is sufficient in itself (i.e., does not require reason) to influence behavior, because the expressive displays of social models in electronic media are directly accessible to the audience via the process of knowledge by acquaintance: the direct pickup of emotional expressions (EII). Buck suggests that humans are biologically constructed to receive certain emotional displays and to understand their meanings directly and without the need for rational processing. He cites evidence that expressive displays have direct effects on viewers that are independent of attitudinal preferences.

Thus, spontaneous cues such as the facial expressions of advertising models support vicarious learning strategies that result in emotion concerning the emotional benefits of advertised brands. Moreover, such observational learning is apt to be greater in television, due to its lifelike representation of human interaction. Marshall McLuhan (1964) also considered television to be a "re-action" (p. 320) medium in the sense that viewers tend to pay greater attention to the facial expressions of the actors than to the action in progress. Accordingly, I suggest that vicarious learning strategies are best achieved through electronic media, which present the facial expressions and other displays of advertising models in more vivid, lifelike, and dynamic images than print and, thereby, produce greater emotion.

PRODUCT-INDUCED AFFECT

Strategies of product-induced affect are different from classical conditioning strategies that derive ad-induced affect from the presentational elements of the ad. Instead, product-induced strategies in ads depict the affect that is derived from the product itself. Certain products, such as ice cream, candy, beer, and sodas, are low in utilitarian (or rational) value but can still be considered to be high in involvement because they are high in pleasure (or emotional) value. The advertising of such products elicits product-induced affect by delineating the pleasure that can be derived from (or the *dis*pleasure that can be removed by!) the advertised brand in a hedonic product category. Therefore, product-induced affect strategies should be associated with greater emotional responses than rational responses.

Involvement here is increased by the use of emotional treatments, which enhance the perceived value of the product. For instance, ads today for certain types of products, like pharmaceuticals, gain their effect by depicting pain and then suggesting relief from the pain through the use of the advertised brand. It was also suggested in chapter 4 that certain products such as automobiles and personal computers are high in rational (importance) value *and* high in pleasure value. The advertising of such products emphasizes systematic learning and *also* elicits product-induced affect by delineating the enjoyment that can be derived from the advertised product. In addition, ads for such products may utilize classical conditioning strategies to derive "ad-induced affect." Product-induced affect in this category serves to increase consumers' existing high involvement whereas systematic learning strategies and ad-induced affect strategies serve to differentiate the advertised brand from competition. An obvious failing of the FCB grid (see below) is its contention that products like automobiles are purchased solely on "thinking." A cursory look at auto ads on TV will reveal the consistent use of "feeling" techniques through spontaneous communication cues like jingles, along with product attributes.

The implication for advertisers is clear. For products with high inherent pleasure value, ads should show the affect that can be derived from the product; for products with low pleasure value, ads should produce ad-induced affect from the presentational elements in the ad, because such products lack the inherent motivational potential to produce affect. In either case, spontaneous communication, using nonverbal cues, is always relevant. Moreover, as emphasized throughout, such communication is best achieved through the broadcast media, which present sensory information in more vivid, lifelike, and dynamic images than print and, thus produce greater emotional response.

THE ADVERTISING DIFFERENTIATION MATRIX

As shown in Table 5.1, the FCB grid (Vaughn, 1980) uses two dimensions to classify products—the level of involvement, ranging from high to low, and a continuum from thinking to feeling. However, the operational measures of thinking and feeling have been seen to load on the same factor as involvement (Vaughn, 1986), suggesting that involvement may be a higher order theoretical construct that encompasses both emotional and rational modes of processing. Park and Young (1986) confirm this when describing affective and cognitive *types* of involvements. More recently, Rossiter, Percy, and Donovan (1991) have also discussed the

TABLE 5.1   The FCB Grid

	Thinking	Feeling
HIGH INVOLVEMENT	1. Informative	2. Affective
LOW INVOLVEMENT	3. Habit Formation	4. Self-Satisfaction

From Vaughn, Richard. (1980), How advertising works: A planning model. Reprinted from the *Journal of Advertising Research*, © Copyright 1980, by the Advertising Research Foundation.

correlation between involvement and thinking-feeling. Contrary to the FCB grid, I maintain that involvement is *both* thinking and feeling, emotion and reason.

Further, it has been pointed out (Pechmann & Stewart, 1989) that feeling and thinking are separate and independent dimensions that cannot realistically be used as opposite ends of a single continuum. In other words, it is entirely possible that a product can be capable of simultaneously eliciting *both* emotional and rational responses. Thus, the Advertising Differentiation Matrix will attempt to classify a large number of product categories on *separate* emotional and rational dimensions.

Figure 5.1 presents an Advertising Differentiation Matrix that uses rational and emotional values to categorize products into four classes. The general implication for advertising strategies that derive from this conceptual approach is that *affective advertising strategies are viable for all product categories*. For instance, ad-induced affect (classical conditioning) can be used in all four classes. Also, vicarious learning and product-induced affect strategies can be used for all products that are high in emotional/pleasure value.

EMOTIONAL VALUE

	LO	HI
HI **RATIONAL VALUE**	2. Industrial Products, Appliances, Banks **Strategy:** Brand Differentiation Classical Conditioning	1. Autos, Airlines, Televisions **Strategy:** Brand Differentiation Product-Induced Affect Classical Conditioning Vicarious Learning
LO	3. Tissues, Fabric Softeners, Detergents **Strategy:** Classical Conditioning Heuristic Learning	4. Candy, Yogurt, Beer, Sodas **Strategy:** Classical Conditioning Product-Induced Affect Vicarious Learning Heuristic Learning

FIGURE 5.1   Advertising Differentiation Matrix.

Quadrant 1

Certain products, such as automobiles, airlines, and televisions, are high in rational value *and* high in emotional value. The advertising of such products emphasizes systematic learning via print media in order to engender rational processing and also elicits product-induced affect by delineating, via broadcast media, the enjoyment that can be derived from the advertised product. Or, vicarious learning strategies in broadcast media may be used in order to depict the social rewards of using the correct brand. In addition, ads for such products can utilize classical conditioning strategies to derive ad-induced affect. Thus, brand information and ad-induced affect *both* serve to differentiate the advertised brand from competition. An obvious failing of the FCB grid (Vaughn, 1980, 1986) is its contention that products like automobiles are purchased solely on "thinking." A cursory look at auto ads on TV will reveal the insistent use of "feeling" techniques for such product categories.

Quadrant 2

Industrial products, services like banking, and household appliances are low in emotional value and high in rational value. The advertising of such products emphasizes systematic learning via the print media. In addition, ads for such products can utilize classical conditioning strategies through symbols and the like to derive ad-induced affect and, thereby, differentiate the advertised brand. The attempt is to generate emotional value through the *advertising* of a product, which otherwise possesses very little inherent affective potential.

Quadrant 3

The FCB grid does not accommodate products that may be low in both thinking and feeling, but certain products, such as tissues, fabric softeners, and detergents, are low in emotional value *and* low in rational value. Ads for such products utilize heuristic learning strategies (use of celebrities, etc.) that provide consumers with easy decision rules for choosing among brands in a low involvement product category. Further, classical conditioning strategies are used, especially through the broadcast media, to derive ad-induced affect, thereby differentiating the brand from competition.

At first glance, it would appear that products in quadrants 2 and 3 could not possibly benefit from emotional advertising. However, ads for industrial products do not just develop beliefs and ads for tissues do not just repeat the brand name (Krugman, 1965). In both classes there is classical conditioning through the subtle use of *symbols*. The attempt is to create involvement *with the ad* by using, say, puppies in an ad for toilet tissues or a parent and child bonding scene for an ad for a bank. Kiddie and canine commercials accounted for a third of the top 25 most popular commercials of 1987 (Alsop, 1988). Affection for trade characters (Snuggle, Pillsbury Doughboy, etc.) also translates into affection for the product.

Quadrant 4

Certain products, such as chocolate, alcoholic beverages, and sodas, are high in emotional value but low in rational value. The advertising of such products uses product-induced affect strategies, especially via broadcast media, which present sensory information using vivid, lifelike, and dynamic images. Product-induced affect strategies delineate the pleasure that can be derived from the advertised product and serve to increase consumers' existing involvement with these products. Unlike the FCB grid, the matrix does not consider these categories to be low involvement. Involvement here can also be increased by the use of other emotional treatments, such as vicarious learning, which enhance the perceived value of the product. Further, actual differences are hard to come by in these products, and advertising is the "real" difference induced through classical conditioning and vicarious learning strategies. Lastly, because such products lack rational value on the level of brand differences, heuristic learning strategies may be employed in order to provide consumers with relatively simple criteria for brand choice.

In sum, high involvement products (high in both emotional and rational values) use product-induced affective strategies *and* brand differentiation strategies. Low involvement products use only ad-induced affective strategies because they lack the capacity to give pleasure from the product and must produce pleasure from the ad. Thus, pleasure is always relevant!

We see, then, that the Advertising Differentiation Matrix has certain definite advantages over the FCB grid in terms of classifying products and depicting the strategies that are best in advertising situations for these products. Overall, the ADM sees emotion and reason as separate dimensions (which comprise the totality of what is called involvement) so that products can be high on both *or* low on both.

RESEARCH RESULTS[2]

A Study of Advertising

In this section I describe a large and comprehensive study of advertisements that incorporates some of the concepts in this and previous chapters. The effects of media, product, and advertising strategy variables on consumers' thoughts and feelings are investigated in the study. Both direct and indirect paths from the advertising variables to ad persuasiveness are also analyzed with the indirect paths leading through affective and cognitive responses. Two hundred and forty television and magazine

---

[2] This research was published in Chaudhuri, Arjun. 1996. The effect of media, product and message factors on ad persuasiveness: The role of affect and cognition. *Journal of Marketing Communications, 2*(4), 201–218.

ads were analyzed with respect to advertising variables, affect, cognition, and ad persuasiveness. The results of the study indicate that advertising variables are indirectly linked to ad persuasiveness, with the indirect path occurring through affective and cognitive responses.

Marketing textbooks usually show a basic communications model in which sender/stimulus effects impact on a receiver. Three important stimulus factors that constitute such effects in marketing communications are media, product, and message (Howard & Sheth, 1969; Klapper, 1960; Zaichkowsky, 1986). However, the effects of media, product, and message factors are typically studied separately in marketing and advertising research. This study examines the simultaneous effects of media, product, and message variables in marketing communications, specifically advertising, and notes the individual contributions of each variable to affective, cognitive, and persuasive outcomes. Obviously this is of critical concern to advertisers, especially if affective and cognitive responses are also related to positive or negative evaluations of the persuasiveness of the ads. Further, the effects of these factors on both affective and cognitive responses are investigated (most studies address only one or the other) and the present study also examines the effects of the advertising variables on the persuasiveness of advertisements. Additionally, the multidimensional affective responses (positive, negative, and reptilian affect) are considered in this study, in contrast to a preference in most advertising studies to examine positive affective responses alone. Lastly, instead of persons as the unit of analysis, this study uses a fairly large number (N = 240) of advertisements as the units of analysis; therefore, the findings of the study should be of greater interest than usual to practitioners of marketing communications, who have to address issues relevant to individual advertisements rather than individual consumers.

Two Routes to Persuasion

Advertising researchers have concerned themselves in recent years with affective and cognitive responses to advertising. Two routes to persuasion have been advocated: a central route that is thoughtful, analytic, and cognitive and a peripheral route that is holistic, synthetic, and affective in nature (Petty & Cacioppo, 1986). Thus, affective and cognitive responses are generally considered today to be the principal mediators of the effects of advertising strategies on persuasive outcomes derived through advertising (Batra & Ray, 1986; Holbrook & Batra, 1987). Accordingly, the following research questions motivated the present study:

RQ1: Do the factors of media, product, and message strategy evoke affective and cognitive responses to television and magazine advertisements?

RQ2: Do these advertising variables directly affect the persuasiveness of the advertisements or are they indirectly linked to ad persuasiveness through affective and cognitive responses?

Measures

Affect and Cognition

Affect and cognition were measured by a multidimensional scale consisting of four subscales; of these, one subscale contained cognitive items and the other three subscales asked for affective responses on the dimensions of positive, negative, and reptilian feelings (see Table 5.2). The scale was a seven-point paper and pencil scale anchored at two ends by "Not at All" and "A Lot." The general form of the scale was "Did the ad make you think about/feel . . .". In all there were 13 items.

With regard to cognitive responses, the operationalization was confined to responses that might be elicited by brand differentiation strategies in advertising. Brand differentiation strategies have repeatedly been found to be the single most important executional factor that influences ad evaluation (Stewart & Furse, 1986; Stewart & Koslow, 1989).

Persuasion

The ad persuasiveness items were drawn from past research in the advertising area (Burton & Lichtenstein, 1988; Edell & Burke, 1987). The items were:

1. Was the ad convincing?
2. Was the ad effective?
3. Was the ad persuasive?

TABLE 5.2   Affective and Cognitive Dimensions in the Study

Positive Affect

Happy

Proud

Hopeful

Sense of Affiliation

Negative Affect

Angry

Disgusted

Irritated

Reptilian Affect

Sexy

Aggressive

Envious

Cognition

Pros and cons of the brand

Facts about the brand

Real differences between the brand and its competitors

Message Strategy

The "objectively observable attributes" (Sewall & Sarel, 1986, p. 53) of the ads were used to measure the message strategies of interest. Table 5.3 lists these items, which were rated using a unipolar seven-point rating scale, anchored by the points "None" and "A Lot." The items in Table 5.3 were compiled from previous studies of advertising content (Haley, Richardson, & Baldwin, 1984; McEwen & Leavitt, 1976; Pechmann & Stewart, 1989; Stewart & Furse, 1986; Stewart & Koslow, 1989).

The attempt here has been to measure some of the ad strategies that may be related to affect and cognition. In particular, family appeals were chosen because it is reasonable to expect that such appeals may be related to the positive affect subscale. Similarly, spokesperson strategies and status appeals may also be expected to relate to affect, whereas product information strategies should be related to cognition. Note that only those advertising elements that could conceivably be in both magazines and television were used. Music, for example, was not assessed as an element because the attempt was to identify the variance that is accounted for by advertising elements that are common to both media and also to identify the variance that is due to the unique nature of each medium. The effect of music, for instance, was included in the unique contribution, if any, made by television as a medium in the study.

TABLE 5.3   Advertising Strategy Items and Rater Reliabilities

Item	Alpha
Product Information	
1. Extent of tangible brand benefits	0.91
2. Extent of ingredients/components	0.92
Spokesperson	
3. Extent of a typical customer	0.94
4. Extent of spokesperson	0.86
5. Extent of user satisfaction	0.79
Family Appeal	
6. Extent of family appeal	0.98
7. Extent of children	0.97
8. Extent of elderly people	0.86
Status Appeal	
9. Extent of affluent setting	0.97
10. Extent of desirable lifestyle	0.87
11. Extent of status appeal	0.84

Product Involvement

The level of product involvement for each of the 29 product categories in the total sample of ads was determined by the Revised Personal Involvement Inventory Scale constructed by Zaichkowsky (1987). The scale provides 10 semantic differential items, which can be summed together to provide one involvement score for each product category. Table 5.4 provides these items along with reliabilities for each product category.

Nature of the Stimuli

This study used ads, rather than individuals, as the units of observation. This method of analysis has been in vogue in recent years (Holbrook & Batra, 1987; Olney, Holbrook, & Batra, 1991; Stewart & Furse, 1986), because it has more significance for advertising practitioners who have to consider the effects of individual ads. Accordingly, 240 advertisements were selected for analysis. Of these, exactly half were television ads and half were print ads from magazines.

The length of TV ads was as follows: 87 of the ads were 30 seconds, 25 were 60 seconds, 3 were 15 seconds, 3 were 90 seconds, 1 was 120 seconds, and 1 was 150 seconds. Print ads were all full-page ads and, of these, two were in black and white and the rest were in color. Ads were selected to represent a range of product categories in both print and TV (see Table 5.5). Ads in both media were also selected to represent, as far as possible, the range of advertising strategies discussed earlier.

Subjects and Procedures

Endogenous Variables

One hundred and twenty-nine undergraduate subjects (64 male, 65 female) provided affective, cognitive, and ad persuasiveness responses, using self-reports, for the entire set of ads. Each subject viewed 10 television ads and

TABLE 5.4   Revised Personal Involvement Inventory (Zaichkowsky, 1987)

Important to me/Unimportant to me

Boring to me/Interesting to me

Relevant to me/Irrelevant to me

Exciting to me/Unexciting to me

Means nothing to me/Means a lot to me

Appealing to me/Unappealing to me

Fascinating to me/Mundane to me

Worthless to me/Valuable to me

Involving to me/Uninvolving to me

Not needed by me/Needed by me

TABLE 5.5 **Product Categories and Ads in the Study**

Product	# of Print Ads	# of TV Ads	Total # of Ads
Autos	11	14	25
Candy	10	7	17
Sneakers	6	2	8
Appliances	2	2	4
Coffee	6	6	12
Cereal	7	4	11
Diamonds	2	2	4
Insurance	3	4	7
Beer	7	8	15
Dental products	3	4	7
Soft drinks	7	11	18
Airlines	6	3	9
Long distance	4	4	8
Household cleaners	4	4	8
Laundry products	4	2	6
Batteries	3	4	7
Wine	2	1	3
Paper products	2	2	4
Fast food	3	5	8
Snack foods	2	1	3
Credit cards	4	5	9
Camera film	6	6	12
Deodorants	2	2	4
Bath soap	2	2	4
Greeting cards	3	3	6
Pharmaceuticals	4	5	9
Personal computers	1	1	2
Express mail	2	4	6
Pet foods	2	2	4
	120	120	240

read 10 magazine ads and provided their response after each ad. A minimum of 10 subjects responded to each ad with regard to affect and cognition and ad persuasiveness. Subjects were randomly assigned to the groups and received course credit for their participation. Half of the questionnaires were reverse ordered to control for order effects, and the order of presentation was also varied by medium by reversing the order of the ads for half the subjects in each group.

Exogenous Variables

Eight judges (four male and four female students in an upper-level advertising class) were trained to rate the extent of the presence of the four advertising strategies, and all eight raters rated 40 (20 for TV and 20 for print) of the 240 ads. The mean of each item for every ad was derived from the scores by the individual raters; this mean was then assigned as the score for that item for the corresponding ad. Note that the study used separate and independent samples of "judges" to arrive at the aggressive measures for the independent and dependent variables attributed to the ads. This is an extremely important precaution that guards against the kind of response bias that is likely to occur when the same sample provides both sets of measures.

For the same reason, a separate sample of 71 undergraduate subjects (30 male, 41 female) responded to each of the 10 product involvement items for 29 product categories in the study. The mean of each of the items for each product category was calculated and then assigned to each ad according to the product that it represented. Thus, each ad was assigned a score on each of the involvement items.

The final analysis used advertisements as the unit of analysis (N = 240), and each ad was provided a mean score (compiled by using the mean of the individual subject's scores, as discussed earlier) to represent the level of affect, cognition, and ad persuasiveness. Similarly, as also discussed earlier, the mean of each ad strategy item was compiled from the individual ratings by the judges who rated the ads for advertising content. Further, each ad was dummy coded to represent television and print media (0 = print, 1 = TV) and product involvement was compiled for all 240 ads.

Results

Covariance structure analysis (using LISREL VII) was employed to test direct and indirect paths from the four advertising strategies to the measures of ad persuasiveness, with the indirect paths occurring through affect and cognition, as measured by the four subscales. Media and product involvement were treated as single indicator variables, assumed to be measured without error.

a. None of the advertising variables were directly linked to ad persuasiveness.
b. All the advertising variables were directly related to one or more of the affective and cognitive constructs. The choice of medium was significantly related to positive effect. This and other media were significantly related to positive affect. This and other results

will be discussed in more detail in the next section. The level of product involvement was positively related to cognition and also to the positive and reptilian aspects of affect. Product information strategies were positively related to cognition. Product information was also negatively related to positive affect and reptilian feelings. Spokesperson strategies were positively related to negative affective reactions, indicating that the use of spokespersons increases negative responses from consumers. Spokesperson strategies also predicted an absence of reptilian and positive feelings. Family appeals were negatively related to reptilian feelings but they were not related to other affects or cognition. Finally, status appeals were positively related to both negative and reptilian affects. These findings are discussed at length later in the Discussion section.

  c. All the affective and cognitive constructs were related to ad persuasiveness. Cognition was strongly and positively (.512) related to ad persuasiveness. The positive dimension of affect was also strongly and positively (.725) related to ad persuasiveness, while the negative and reptilian affect subscales were negatively related to ad persuasiveness.

    Thus, it follows from a, b, and c that all the advertising variables (media, product, message) in the study were indirectly related to ad persuasiveness, with the indirect path occurring through affect and cognition.

    As Figure 5.2 shows, the generation of greater cognitive thinking about brands was not due to differences in the media used in the study but due to differences in the levels of involvement with the product category advertised and the levels of product information provided by an advertisement. In fact, the results show that advertisements using high involvement products are capable of provoking both thoughts and feelings. If we accept that affect and cognition constitute "involvement" at the time of advertising exposure (or ad involvement), then there is evidence in this study that the level of pre-existing involvement with the product category (or product involvement) was significantly and positively related to both cognitive and affective (positive and reptilian) dimensions. Ads for high involvement products lead to involvement with the ad which, in turn, leads to a positive or negative evaluation of the ad.

    The findings also indicate that spokesperson strategies create negative reactions such as anger, disgust, and irritation. Spokespeople, typical consumers relating satisfaction with their products, are also strongly conducive to an absence of positive affective responses such as happiness, pride, and hope. This does not necessarily suggest that spokesperson strategies are ineffective. These strategies may still be effective in terms of other measures (say "recall") of advertising effectiveness, which were not examined in this

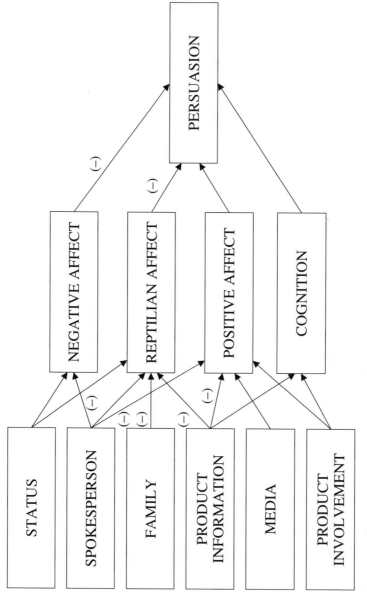

FIGURE 5.2   Final (Trimmed) Model.

study. However, if the intention of the advertiser is to create a positive emotional bond between the consumer and the product, then the results of this study advise against the use of spokespeople in ads. Perhaps this advertising format has become all too common and suffers from "wear out" so that spokespeople evoke negative responses from consumers.

Although status appeals were not significantly related to the cognitive or positive affect dimensions, there was a positive and significant relationship with negative and reptilian affects. Note also that both negative and reptilian affects were negatively related to ad persuasiveness. Thus, it is recommended that advertisers regularly assess their campaigns in terms of negative and reptilian affect responses. "Emotional" ads are widely used today and large sums of money are appropriated for "image" campaigns, but advertisers may not be completely cognizant of the range of negative and reptilian affective experiences that their ads evoke.

Product information strategies generate cognition and discourage the occurrence of positive and reptilian affects. These findings are in keeping with prior research. For instance, these findings corroborate the Fishbein model of reasoned action in which beliefs generate active information processing. However, family appeals were not positively related to any of the affective aspects and predicted only the absence of reptilian affects. Perhaps family appeals work in conjunction with other appeals like nostalgia, special occasions, and the like in order to produce positive affect.

Most importantly, there is considerable evidence in this study that affect and cognition mediate the effect of advertising strategies on measures of ad persuasiveness. None of the ad strategies were directly related to ad persuasiveness, yet all were directly related to affect and cognition, which, in turn, were all related to ad persuasiveness. These findings corroborate the work of Holbrook and Batra (1987), and the present study extends their findings in the context of a larger number of ads, ads from both television and print, both affect and cognition, both positive and negative feelings, and a more rigorous causal modeling approach that simultaneously examines the effect of advertising strategies on a number of different variables.

Limitations of the Study

The generalization of the findings of this study must be made with caution and thoughtfulness. The student population from which subjects were drawn largely tends to be a homogenous one in terms of income, occupation, age, and such other nontheoretical aspects. Thus, this helps control for such variables and strengthens the internal validity of the study. However, such a population is not entirely representative of the world of consumers that advertising deals with, and thus this weakens the external validity or generalizability of the findings. At the same time, such a population may well and truly represent a population of human beings in terms of the very basic psychological responses that have been the subject of this study. Accordingly, the aggregate data extracted from student subjects may not deviate considerably from aggregate data collected from other populations.

In the same manner, judgment must be exercised in understanding and accepting the experimental conditions under which the present study was conducted. Subjects were exposed to ads under "forced exposure" conditions in which they were *required* to watch/read the ads. In a natural viewing situation, consumers may not pay so much attention to advertising and results may be different. The objective in this study has been to determine relationships within the closely controlled, perhaps even artificial, conditions of the laboratory. The task for the advertising practitioner is to determine if the same principles that have been established in the laboratory hold under natural conditions and under conditions that are peculiar to individual circumstances. Replication of the present study under different conditions is recommended before applying its findings to individual cases.

Further, note that the advertisements in the study were drawn from a selected sample of ads and did not constitute a random sample. This also places limits on the generalizability of the results. A selected sample was necessary in order to successfully manipulate the independent variables in the study, as discussed in an earlier section. It should be remembered, however, that all ads used in the study were actual ads from actual campaigns. No "artificiality" was introduced in this case through the use of mock ads, for instance.

Note also that the study makes *no* conclusions concerning the sales of products based on the results of the study. Advertising effectiveness has been measured in terms of certain psychological responses and not in terms of purchase indicators. The connections between these psychological variables and attitudinal indicators and purchase intentions has been the subject of earlier research and continues to vex theorists and practitioners alike.

6

PERSONALITY AND THE SELF

Seems, madam! Nay it is; I know not 'seems.'
'Tis not alone my inky cloak, good mother, . . .
That can denote me truly: these indeed seem,
For they are actions that a man might play:
But I have that within which passeth show;
These but the trappings and the suits of woe.

(Hamlet, I, 2)

The inability of Shakespeare's man in black to externalize his grief in action, rather than in words, is well known. Mysteriously enough, the soldier-scholar is temporarily struck down by a terrible sorrow that releases itself not in any act of vengeance, but in soul-searching agony. Hamlet, like all of us when numbed by emotion, strives to evaluate his inner self. It is only when he comes to terms with his self that his sadness leaves him and he is able to return as a man of action.

Self-concept theorists will understand exactly why the prince takes five long acts to make up his famous mind. The discrepancies in the protagonist's self-concept among his actual self (represented by his present state of inaction), his ideal self (the tenets of conventional morality), and his ought self (the demands of a pagan Nordic tradition) need to be reconciled and accepted in self-knowledge. Only then can his emotional distress be alleviated. The internal conflict raging in Hamlet's mind can also be interpreted as strife between the rational and the emotional, or between the dual selves of the ego and the id. The outcome of this torment is self-evaluation and self-knowledge because, to quote Willeford (1987), "all knowledge of the self is emotional" (p. 42). The same connection was made by Jung in 1907, when he wrote, "the essential basis of our personality is affectivity" (in Willeford, 1987, p. 42).

This chapter will attempt to find a relationship between emotional communication and some aspects of the self-concept. The role of affective interaction in determining persons' notions of self has not had much direct evaluation. The literature on both emotion and self-concept is, of course, legion and the role of affect in interpersonal relations is also well documented (deRivera, 1984; Kelly, 1984). There has been work on external feedback and self-inconsistencies (Swann, 1983) and also on self-discrepancies, which result in negative emotional outcome (Higgins, 1987). Without making light of the notion that self-beliefs lead to emotional behavior, it is suggested that social interaction via emotional communication may determine beliefs and concepts of the self.

EMOTION AND SELF-CONCEPT

Personality is a set of inferences about a person and determines the person's behavior. The self-concept is one construct among the system of constructs that define personality such as habits, sentiments (feelings, affects, emotions), cognitions, traits, and behavior styles. Two aspects of the self that are generally indicative of a person's self-concept are the social and private selves (Wylie, 1968). Discrepancies between the self-states arise out of cognitive *and* affective evaluation, and certain discrepancies have been associated with negative emotions, such as sadness, fear, and anger (Higgins, 1987). Zajonc (1980) also states that affects clearly implicate the self and affective judgments describe "something that is in ourselves" (p. 157).

The *private self* is a person's perceptions of his or her ability to control the environment. These perceptions can range from extremes of high confidence and high self-worth in the presence of others to utter helplessness and feelings of inadequacy. The *social self* is a person's perception of his or her desire for social interaction and can range from extremes of extroverted gregariousness to introverted social inhibitions and misanthropic inclinations to shun the company of others. These definitions do not attempt to preclude other conceptualizations and are by no means meant to be exhaustive and completely comprehensive. For instance, no attempt has been made to include the perceptions of individuals about the social roles that they play (Goffman, 1959).

Without making light of the notion that our self-concept leads to emotional behavior, it is suggested here that social interaction via emotional communication may also determine beliefs and concepts of the self. According to Higgins (1987), a person's notions of their actual social competence, when contrasted with their ideals, account for emotional discomfort and neurosis. This represents emotion as an outcome of self-concept via the route of cognitive evaluation. The possibility must also be considered that self-concept is, in turn, a direct outcome of negative and positive emotions generated through social interaction.

Our present understanding of the effect of the social environment on self-concept has a long and illustrious history. According to Cooley (1902), the self is constructed by taking the perspective of others, as through a "looking glass" (p. 183), and James (1890) states that "a man's Social Self is the recognition that he gets from his mates" (p. 294). This notion of the self as learned from others is clarified further by Mead (1934) in his determination of the "generalized other" (p. 154), which is seen as "the attitude of the whole community" (p. 154) with which the individual interacts.

Thus, the self understands itself through its conception (correct or otherwise) of the attitudes of various social groups towards the individual, and this accounts for the many selves/roles that may be played. Moreover, the self, though sensitive to modifications, does not keep changing constantly, but has stability and at least a semi-permanent structure. Webster and Sobieszek (1974) summarized the research on the self and concluded that the opinions of others are a critical determinant of the self and the significance of others is "a direct function of the frequency of interaction with those others" (p. 28). Carl Rogers (1951) also emphasizes that the self is formed as a result of the environment and interaction with others and that its structure is "organized, fluid, but consistent" (p. 498).

It should be noted that Mead's (1934) symbolic interactionist viewpoint on the self is that of a conscious, controlled, *cognitive* process and quite contrary to the Freudian, psychoanalytic position, which maintains that the self is primarily a function of innate characteristics and tendencies of the individual. In this developmental theory of the self, although the ego does mediate between the id and its environment (Freud, 1961), the self is seen as prior to the social process. To the interactionist, however, comprehensive understanding of the emotion process as a social feedback device may reconcile both developmental and interactionist points of view of the self.

EMOTIONAL COMMUNICATION AND THE SELF

We have seen that there are three readouts of emotional-motivational states: adaptive/homeostatic response, spontaneous expression, and subjective experience (affect). The individual, when sufficiently provoked by internal or external stimuli, is capable of manifesting these states in all three ways simultaneously, but independently. Motivational/emotional states take the form of neurochemical activity, and lead to both the subjective experience of emotion and spontaneous, involuntary communication by way of facial expressions, postures, and the like. The responses of others (say, during puberty) to such spontaneous expression provide emotional education that helps the individual to understand and label his or her subjective experience of feelings and desires.

This emotional education involves the integration of "raw" subjective experience with learned, structured rules of expression (display rules) and comes to define an essential aspect of the self—the "self-as-description."

The "self-as-acquaintance" (Buck, 1988, p. 448), on the other hand, is derived directly from the immediate experience of feelings, desires, and so on, and resists description. However, it is the raw material that through the attribution process of cognitive labeling and appraisal results in the self as an object of description.

Thus, the innate tendencies of the "developmental self" find expression in emotional feeling and emotional communication, and this, in turn, is made linguistically meaningful through feedback that results in the formation of the "looking glass" or "interactionist self." The implication is clear: There are two routes to the self, one through the direct experience of emotion and the other through a learned, conscious, and cognitive process of emotional education. Emotional communication is the link between others and the self.

As depicted in Figure 6.1, the process of emotional communication begins with a stimulus that evokes a physiological response in terms of neurochemical and autonomic nervous system activity. This is consonant with Zajonc's (1980) view that the affective is the first level of response to the environment and governs the subsequent relations with the stimulus. Zajonc (1980) and Buck (1988) confirm that a stimulus can impinge directly on emotional systems without cognitive mediation. If this state of arousal is acutely felt and consciously attended to, it simultaneously but independently results in spontaneous expression and the subjective experience of the emotion. These are tempered by the display rules proper for behavior, as indicated by a cognitive appraisal, labeling, and understanding of the stimulus. This cognitive interpretation, in turn, is influenced by the individual differences in one's "developmental history" (Buck, 1988, p. 27), such as memories of past learning experiences *and* unique personality traits *including* a generalized notion of the self. Thus, the same stimulus can cause different emotional interpretations across persons (Roseman, 1984), depending on differences in innate and learned characteristics.

This complex interaction of emotion, cognition, and personality has consequences for the self-concept. Higgins (1987) shows that any resultant discrepancies between the self-states cause further emotional activity. Moreover, the developmental history of the person is updated and affects future appraisal of stimuli. Thus, the relationship between emotion and self-concept is seen as reciprocal, ongoing, and exchange-oriented. Individuals make attributions concerning their self-concept based on emotional interactions, and then communicate emotionally on the basis of the derived self-concept. The self-concept is updated based on the frequency of emotional incidents with others and, conversely, according to the attributions made by the self, the frequency of emotional interaction with others increases or decreases. Such a theory of interactive yet independent systems of emotion, cognition, and self-concept serves to bridge the differences, reviewed earlier, among some of the theories of emotion, social

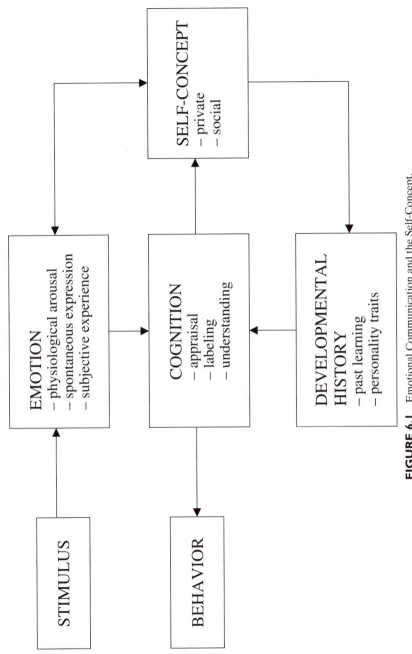

FIGURE 6.1   Emotional Communication and the Self-Concept.

relations, and the self. Thus, psychosocial, psychophysiological, and cognitive theories of emotion describe different parts of a complex process; Freudian and symbolic interactionist positions describe different aspects of the self, one learned from others, the other known directly through subjective emotional experience; and communication, sociological, and psychological perspectives together account for a fuller representation of human behavior.

IMPLICATIONS FOR MARKETING

What implications does the theory of the self-concept have for marketing? Are there products that enhance both the private and social self-concepts? Are there message strategies that can be rooted in improving consumers' self-esteem ("*others* will think well of you if you use brand X" or "*you* will think better of yourself if you use this brand")? The entire notion of healthy foods and health-oriented services is based on improving consumers' private and social self-concepts, is it not? The tricky part is deciding whether to appeal to the private or the social self! Can you find out which is more important to your target market segment?

The management of sales personnel may benefit from such an interpretation of the role of emotion in self-concept. The implication is that salespersons' self-concepts are derived from both the emotional experiences they encounter on the job and the *feedback* they receive about such experiences from their supervisors. If you are the supervisor, what feedback will you provide when you see a depressed salesperson? Or an angry one? Frustrated? Anxious? And how about the guy who is always joking around? Your reactions are as critical to their success as their own personalities.

RESEARCH RESULTS

Purpose of the Study

This study attempted to find a relationship between emotional communication and some aspects of the self-concept. I attempted to relate the frequency of emotional interaction with self-reported feelings of inadequacy and social inhibitions. In particular, I attempted to derive a link between positive *and* negative *affective* interaction and positive and negative self-concept.

Referring back to Mead (1934) and Rogers (1951), we are reminded that the self has a semi-permanent, organized, and consistent structure. Jones and Pittman (1982) imply this structure is capable of description by subjects when they write that "each of us has a potentially available overarching cognition of his or her interrelated dispositions . . . the notion of a phenomenal self implies that memories of past actions and outcomes are available in integrated form" (p. 232). Accordingly, the *self-as-description* may be viewed as a person's *self-reported* awareness of his or her private and social selves.

As discussed before, the *private self* is a person's perceptions of his or her ability to control the environment. These perceptions can range from extremes of high confidence and high self-worth in the presence of others to utter helplessness and feelings of inadequacy. The *social self* is a person's perception of his or her desire for social interaction and can range from extremes of extroverted gregariousness to introverted social inhibitions and misanthropic inclinations to shun the company of others. The endeavor in this study was to measure some (certainly not all) aspects of the self that are developed through emotional communication in social relations. The private and social selves were operationalized by a set of questions depicting "feelings of inadequacy" and "social inhibitions," respectively. Display rules affect expressive behavior as well as self-reports of emotional experience (Buck, 1988). However, although self-reports are mediated by display rules and organized by language, they are still "observable manifestations of motivation and emotion" (Buck, 1988, p. 29) and thus may provide a valid measure of the cognitive rendering of subjective emotional experience. It is the relationship between appraised, subjective emotional experience during social interaction and the self as known by description that has been investigated through self-reports in this study. The literature reviewed earlier in this paper suggests that such a relationship is entirely possible. Zajonc (1980) also states that affects clearly implicate the self and affective judgments describe "something that is in ourselves" (p. 157).

There is some difference of opinion concerning the primary affects, but in consonance with the theory of social biofeedback, presented earlier, the six universal emotions recorded from facial expressions by Ekman and Friesen (1975) have been accepted as particularly suitable to this study. Shaver, Schwartz, Kirson, and O'Connor (1987) show that there are indeed prototypic or basic emotions that adequately represent a host of other subordinate-level emotions. The same authors also demonstrate that each of the emotion prototypes possesses a unique set of antecedents, behavioral responses, and control procedures, thus vindicating the approach that these are emotional effects that can be assessed independently. The prototypes described by and large confirm the ones established by Ekman and Friesen. Thus, for the purposes of this study, the concept of emotional communication is operationally defined as "the self-reported feelings of the frequency of happiness, sadness, fear, anger, surprise, and disgust that are generated in the presence of others." This operationalization was executed by six questions interspersed in the same questionnaire that measured aspects of the self-concept.

It was predicted that the *greater* the extent of reported negative emotion (sadness, fear, anger, disgust) in the presence of others, the *greater* the feelings of inadequacy and social inhibitions. Further, the *greater* the extent of reported positive emotion (happiness, surprise), the *lesser* the feelings of inadequacy and social inhibition.

Methods

The theoretical approach presented thus far justifies this study's treatment of emotional communication as the independent variable of interest and of certain aspects of the self-concept as the dependent variable. Accordingly, a survey consisting of 40 questions was conducted among 89 undergraduate men and women at a northeastern state university. Subjects completed the questionnaire during the first 20 minutes of various communications classes. Subjects were told that the survey was on social interactions and that all responses were anonymous. The questionnaire consisted of three sets of questions: The first set of 6 questions asked for subjects' perceptions of their frequency of emotional experience in the presence of other people—"How often do you feel happy/sad/afraid/angry/disgusted/surprised in the presence of others?" (Each of these questions constitutes independent variables in the study.) The second set of 23 questions was designed to assess subjects' "feelings of inadequacy" in their social interactions, and responses were compiled in an index to represent the first dependent variable. The last set of 11 questions assessed subjects' social inhibitions, and again an index was compiled to provide the second dependent variable.

The two sets of questions on self-concept were adopted from the Personality Questionnaire designed by Janis and Field (1959), who labeled these sets as "feelings of inadequacy" and "social inhibitions" and used them as measures of self-esteem (p. 55). These five-point self-rating scales were anchored in one of two ways, according to the syntax of the questions: "Very Often . . . Practically Never" and "Very . . . Not At All." Each scale point was assigned a score ranging from 5 to 1, and a subject's total score on each cluster was derived from his or her factor scores on that cluster (see Results). Janis and Field previously demonstrated the reliability of the questions in each cluster by using split half reliability estimates (p. 58).

Results

Factor analysis with an orthogonal two-factor solution (with varimax rotation) was used to derive factor scores for the dependent variables. Each subject thus was assigned a factor score for each dependent variable. In effect, the factor score indices were the new "operational definitions" for each of the dependent variables, and the indices ensured that the variables were orthogonal in that only the independent contributions of each question to each factor were utilized in further analysis. These two factors accounted for 37.7% of the variance in the questions and had eigenvalues of 9.38 and 3.45, respectively. Almost all of the 23 questions in the "feelings of inadequacy" cluster loaded heavily on the first factor (factor loadings of .5 or above) and the pattern was reversed for the second factor, where most of the questions in the "social inhibitions" cluster had strong loadings. This further corroborated the reliability of the Janis and Field questions in measuring two independent dimensions of the self, labeled as "feelings of inadequacy" and "social inhibitions."

Tables 6.1 and 6.2 show the results of stepwise regression analysis that was used to assess the effect of the six emotion items on each of the two dependent variables. Forty-four percent of the variance in "feelings of inadequacy," $F (3,81) = 21.21$, $p < .01$, and 27% of the variance in "social inhibitions," $F (2,82) = 15.49$, $p < .01$, was explained by the independent variables in the final step.

Sadness and fear were positively related to feelings of inadequacy and both were significant at the $p < .01$ level. Surprise had a negative linear relationship with feelings of inadequacy. Happiness, anger, and disgust

TABLE 6.1   Stepwise Multiple Linear Regression: Feelings of Inadequacy as Dependent Variable

Independent Variable	Beta	Significance
Sadness	.5456	$p < .01$
Fear	.3116	$p < .01$
Surprise	−.2156	$p < .05$

R Square = .4398 (final step)
F = 21.19 with 3 and 81 d.f., significant at $p < .01$

Note: Further analysis using orthogonal polynomials showed a significant ($p < .01$) *nonlinear* relationship between surprise and feelings of inadequacy.

TABLE 6.2   Stepwise Multiple Linear Regression: Social Inhibitions as Dependent Variable

Independent Variable	Beta	Significance
Happiness	−.4286	$p < .01$
Surprise	.2362	$p < .05$

R Square = .2742 (final step)
F = 15.48 with 2 and 82 d.f., significant at $p < .01$

failed to achieve significance (p > .05) on feelings of inadequacy. Further analysis using orthogonal polynomials showed a significant (p < .01) *nonlinear* relationship between surprise and feelings of inadequacy. However, happiness in the presence of others had a significant (p < .01) negative relationship with social inhibitions. Although surprise had a significant (p < .05) positive relationship to social inhibitions, all the other emotion items made nonsignificant contributions.

Discussion

The reported frequency of emotional communication in the presence of others can be used to predict self-concept, as measured by self-reports on feelings of inadequacy and social inhibitions. Interestingly, these aspects of the self are seen to have quite different emotional underpinnings. Happiness in the presence of others is predictive of a lack or absence of social inhibitions, but it is not a factor in feelings of inadequacy. Sadness and fear can predict feelings of inadequacy, but do not predict the presence or absence of social inhibitions.

The findings on happiness, sadness, and fear are intuitively plausible. People who do not find happiness in the presence of others tend to be socially inhibited and people who experience sadness and fear in the presence of others tend to have feelings of inadequacy, helplessness, and lack of control over their environment. Shaver et al. (1987) studied the scripts of the basic emotion prototypes and they document that fear accounts provided by subjects began with descriptions of situations potentially harmful to the self - situations of uncertainty, loss, or vulnerability, in which the individual lacks control. deRivera (1984) speaks of fear as denoting change in a relationship, whereby the individual withdraws from the other and focuses on the self. Thus, the accumulated memories of such feelings, with their accompanying physiological responses of sweating, nervousness, and the like, may lead to a lowering of self-esteem and feelings of inadequacy in social relations.

The inconsequential effect of anger on self-concept in this study is difficult to account for and needs to be explored further. However, it is possible that the nature of self-reports inhibits persons' admission of an emotion that they have traditionally been taught to repress and deny. According to Scheff (1984), there is, in general, a prohibition against anger in advanced societies.

The differential effects of surprise are especially noteworthy. Surprise is capable of predicting both aspects of the self, but in quite different ways because it had a significant positive, linear relationship with social inhibitions and a significant nonlinear relationship with feelings of inadequacy. This suggests that surprise can have different effects on the self-concept depending on the extent of its presence. Surprise in the presence of others points to the presence of social inhibitions. Thus, understandably, people who experience large amounts of uncertainty in the environment tend to be cautious and socially inhibited.

The nonlinear, U-shaped form of the relationship between surprise and feelings of inadequacy also confirms that higher amounts of uncertainty may, in certain cases, lead to negative self-esteem. Those people who encounter the unexpected (surprise) repeatedly tend to have feelings of inadequacy and uncertainty in dealing with their social environment. However, it would also appear that people who have had the experience of dealing with moderate amounts of surprise and unexpectedness may have learned to deal effectively with their environment, and this leads to lower feelings of inadequacy and greater confidence in their capability to handle social situations. On the other hand, people who have had little experience with surprising situations have not, as yet, learned to cope with uncertainty in their environment, and this may produce greater feelings of inadequacy in their case.

This study has explored the subject of the self-as-description. The self-as-acquaintance process needs to be addressed in future studies. Can individuals make attributions to their self-concepts directly, by way of subjective experience, without any cognitive evaluation? Obviously self-reports could not be utilized in such studies. Also, experiments would have to be designed (using, say, facial expressions to stimuli or projective tests) with situations in which subjects were not conscious of being observed. Such precautions might avoid display rules but would also preclude the presence of "others." Perhaps audiotaped or written evaluations of subjects could be used.

Future research must also explore the implications for behavior under different conditions. If indeed there are two routes to self-concept—directly by subjective experience and also via a peripheral cognitive routing—then the possibility must also exist for two incompatible attributions affecting the self-concept. Will this result in stress and inaction, as in the case of the Shakespearean hero? Or will cognition overcome the affective response as Swann et al. (1987) suggest? Does it depend on the power of the source of the affect or on the personality of the subject? This study has attempted to show that part of the answer may lie in our emotional interactions with others. Results indicate that the frequency of emotional communication in the presence of others can be used to predict some aspects of the self-concept.

7[1]

RISK

You take a chance on an airplane
You take a chance when you cross the street
You take a chance when you love somebody
When you're standing near the heat

(Bob Seger, 1990)

Researchers have identified two components of risk. The first is the probability of the occurrence of the risk factor ("How likely is it that you will be in an automobile/airplane accident?"). The second is the severity of the consequences of the threat factor ("If you were in an automobile/airplane accident, how bad is the outcome likely to be?"). The two components are usually multiplied together to form an index of risk. As you can see, two risk factors (automobile versus airplane, for example) with the same multiplicative score could involve very different underpinnings for the nature of the risk. In addition to the two components of risk, Jacoby and Kaplan (1972) have identified five different types of risk: financial, performance, social, pyschological, and physical. Two categories of perceived risk ("inherent" and "handled") have also been identified in earlier research (Bettman, 1973; Dowling & Staelin, 1994; Lutz & Reilly, 1974). Inherent risk refers to the risk innate in a product class or product choice, whereas handled risk refers to the risk in the buying situation or brand choice within a product class.

This chapter investigates the relationship among emotion, reason, and perceived risk. It is suggested that emotional factors account for a significant and substantial portion of the variance in perceived risk even after the effect of rational factors (perceived differences between alternatives) has been taken into account. The primary purpose of this chapter is to investigate whether the emotions evoked by consumption of products and services can

---

explain the phenomenon of perceived risk. Such an investigation serves to increase our theoretical understanding of the construct of perceived risk, which has already been linked to important risk reduction behaviors such as information search (Dowling & Staelin, 1994; Srinivasan & Ratchford, 1991). It also fills a critical gap in our present theories of consumer behavior. For instance, in their groundbreaking paper on the experiential aspects of consumption, Holbrook and Hirschman (1982, p. 132) acknowledge in a footnote that they did not account for perceived risk in their theoretical framework depicting the role of emotion in consumer behavior.

Moreover, there has been a preponderance of recent reports in the business media on the theme that people's use of products and services is fraught with feelings of fear, anger, and sadness. Americans feel insecure in airplanes and elevators (Kanner, 1994); shoppers are making fewer shopping trips because of concerns about crime (Garvey, 1994); people feel unsafe in their homes (Fitzgerald, 1994) and in their cars (Parks, 1995); negative feelings afflict 40 million adults in the United States, especially those who are heavy users of alcohol and tobacco products (Crispell, 1993); consumer anxiety leads to choices in car rental insurance (Simmons, 1995), and mortgages (Blumenthal, 1995); Olympic organizers spent $100 million on security (Thomas, 1995). Faced with this environment, it would seem incumbent upon consumer researchers to delve into the antecedents and consequences of emotion in present-day consumption experiences.

Accordingly, a model is presented in this chapter that suggests linkages among product type, emotion, reason, perceived risk, and ongoing search.

EMOTION AND PERCEIVED RISK

In his seminal paper on risk taking, Bauer (1960) enunciated the theme that consumer behavior involves risk in the sense that any action of a consumer will produce consequences that he or she views with some amount of uncertainty. Further, Bauer conceived that consumers develop ways of reducing risk by obtaining information that enables them to act with a degree of confidence in situations of uncertainty. This notion that information reduces risk, uncertainty, and conflict has been addressed in other work as well (Berlyne, 1960; Bettman, 1979). However, in contrast to "rational" information processing theorists, Bauer also noticed that the perception of risk can be "traumatic" for high priced items like automobiles, thus providing us with a clue that emotion and perceived risk are related in some way.

Such a relationship may be explained, at least in part, by referring to the conceptualization of emotion presented in Chapter 1. Emotion and perceived risk are related because emotion is knowledge and knowledge affects risk. Traditionally, we tend to think of knowledge as "cold cognition," or rational information that is processed analytically and that functions to reduce risk and uncertainty. Recall from the earlier discussion, however, that emotion may be conceived of as a type of knowledge as well—knowledge by acquaintance (in contrast to knowledge by description), which is a subjective experience known only by direct acquaintance with phenomena that may serve to provide holistic experiential information about products and services.

Although they may each occur as aspects of the consumption experience, perceived risk is a construct distinct from emotion and rational information. In their model of the antecedents and consequences of overall perceived risk, Dowling and Staelin (1994) present "prior knowledge" with the product category as a determinant of overall perceived risk. Dowling and Staelin conceive of such prior knowledge to consist solely of rational information concerning the attributes (quality, price, etc.) of the product, based on consumers' past experiences with the product. In contrast, it is suggested here that emotion is also an aspect of such prior knowledge with the product category. Consumers engage in experiential encounters with the product category during trials, demonstrations, purchase, and usage of the product. In addition to "rational" knowledge, these experiential encounters also result in knowledge by acquaintance or emotion. Seen in this light, emotion is a determinant of perceived risk (because it may increase or decrease the perception of risk), and perceived risk itself is defined as the overall evaluation of the potential for loss in a product class.

This potential for loss, or perceived risk, is an overall evaluation of the consumer's prior knowledge of the rational and emotional consequences of using a product or service. Emotion, or knowledge by acquaintance, leads to an overall evaluation of the potential for loss because negative emotion raises the potential for loss by pointing out the emotional disadvantages of using the product whereas positive emotion reduces the potential for loss by pointing out the emotional advantages of using the product. Additionally, rational, utilitarian factors such as the importance/relevance of the product to the consumer's life may also contribute to the overall evaluation of risk (Bettman, 1973). Thus, perceived risk is derived from both emotion and reason. Perceptions of risk arise from knowledge about a product and, as described before, emotion and reason account for two different sources of knowledge or information about our environment; one through appraisal (knowledge by description), the other through intuition (knowledge by acquaintance).

In fact, it may be expected that emotion will explain variance in perceived risk in addition to the variance explained by rational/utilitarian factors such as the level of perceived differences between alternative brands in a product or service. According to Zajonc (1980), emotion is, as least in part, independent of reason. Although this view has been hotly debated (Lazarus, 1984; Tsal, 1985), compelling anecdotal and scientific evidence cited by Zajonc and Markus (1982) indicates that rational factors may not account for all of the consumption experience with respect to the perception of risk in products and services. For instance, our fear of flying cannot be overcome by cognition-based arguments. No amount of rational reassurance can dispel that visceral feeling in the gut as the plane accelerates on the runway. Emotion in the consumption experience may indeed be a singular and unique determinant of risk.

A MODEL OF EMOTION AND PERCEIVED RISK

Figure 7.1 depicts a model of the expected linkages between emotion, perceived differences between alternatives in the product/service (reason or cognition), and perceived risk. In addition, certain antecedents of the process are also modeled. In general, it is postulated that the characteristics of a product or service ("utilitarian" and "hedonic" aspects) determine the nature of the rational (perceived differences between alternatives) or emotional response to the product or service, which, in turn, determines the level of overall perceived risk in the product or service. Note that the general structure of the model mirrors established models of advertising effects in which the characteristics of the stimuli (ad or product) affect emotional/rational response, which, in turn, create an overall evaluation of the stimuli and lead to some behavioral outcome. Emotional and rational responses to products and services may together be considered to represent the level of "product involvement" just as these responses are usually considered to represent aspects of "ad involvement" in studies of advertising effects (Park & Young, 1986). Such product involvement is usually considered to be a function of the product itself (Zaichkowsky, 1985, 1986, 1994). Unfortunately, there is no empirical verification in the literature as to what types of products are likely to be more "involving." However, the distinction between hedonic and utilitarian product types has been seen to account for important consumer behavior phenomena (Batra & Ahtola, 1991; Holbrook & Hirschman, 1982) and these categories are, in general, considered to be quintessential product types, akin to the notions of luxuries and necessities (Bearden & Etzel, 1982). Accordingly, these two characteristics of products and services are included as two purely exogenous variables in the model. The hedonic value of a product or service is defined as "the level of pleasure that the product or service is capable of giving to the average consumer" and the utilitarian value of a product or service is defined as "the level of usefulness of the product or service in solving the everyday problems of the average consumer."

The model in Figure 7.1 proposes that the hedonic and utilitarian values of products and services are positively related to the level of perceived differences between alternatives of these products and services; however, products that are high in hedonic value are also positively related to a potential for both positive and negative emotional experiences and

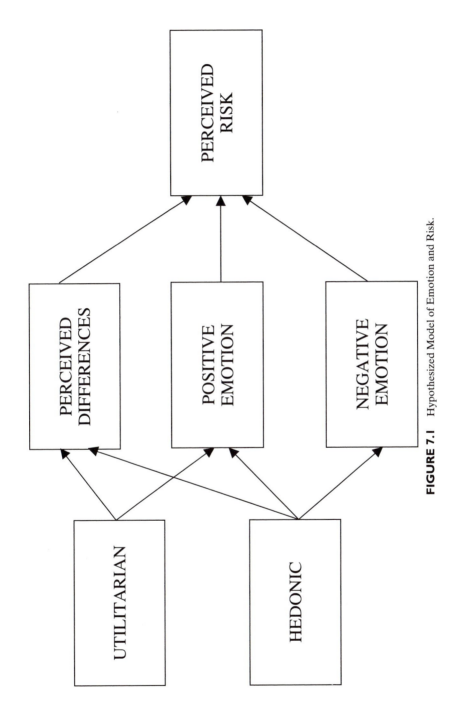

FIGURE 7.1   Hypothesized Model of Emotion and Risk.

perceived risk. These relationships are based on the two main paradigms in consumer behavior theory. The information processing paradigm (Bettman, 1979) regards consumer behavior as largely objective, rational, and problem-solving behavior. Thus, consumers are likely to engage in rational information processing of products that are high in hedonic and utilitarian values as a result of the tangible attributes of these products and services. This results in greater perceptions of perceived differences between alternative brands in products and services.

Television sets, for example, are high in both hedonic and utilitarian values (Laurent & Kapferer, 1985). This motivates consumers to process information about brands, resulting in knowledge about differences among brands of television sets. Such knowledge about significant differences among brands in the product category may further generate perceptions of high perceived risk in the product category.

The experiential paradigm, on the other hand, considers consumer behavior to be the pursuit of subjective, emotional, and symbolic consumption experiences (Holbrook & Hirschman, 1982). Hedonic products and services that have nontangible, symbolic benefits (in addition to tangible benefits) are, thus, likely to be related to a greater potential for both positive and negative emotional consumption experiences. Luxury cars, perfumes, fashion, candy, and alcohol, for instance, may not only provide a great deal of pleasure, but also have the potential for undesirable consequences. Scientists and poets alike have spoken of the pleasure-pain dichotomy in human existence (Freud, 1920). To quote Shelley (1993, p. 39),

> "Our sincerest laughter with some pain is fraught,
> Our sweetest songs are those that tell of saddest thought."

Thus, the extent of hedonic and utilitarian value in products and services is seen to be indirectly related to perceived risk, with the indirect paths leading through perceived differences between alternatives and emotion. Dowling and Staelin (1994), in describing a process model of perceived risk, also model prior knowledge (emotion and reason in our case) as an antecedent of perceived risk. Thus, there is theoretical justification to consider emotion to be a determinant of perceived risk in this study as well.

As discussed earlier, it seems reasonable that positive emotional experiences with products and services decrease the degree of perceived risk whereas negative emotional experiences serve to increase the level of perceived risk. Emotion is knowledge about the hedonic or other emotional values of a product or service, just as information about a product's tangible attributes is knowledge about the functional or utilitarian values of the product or service. Such knowledge may serve to reduce the potential for loss (or perceived risk) in a product or service if the consumption experience usually generates positive feelings. However, if negative feelings persistently occur, then the perception of risk and potential loss will increase. Thus, it may be expected that products and services for which consumers report high levels of negative feelings during the consumption experience will also be associated with high levels of perceived risk. Similarly, products and services for which consumers report low levels of negative feelings will be associated with low levels of perceived risk. In sum, it is expected that there will be a positive relationship between negative emotions and perceived risk.

On the other hand, products and services for which consumers report high levels of positive feelings during consumption should be associated with low levels of perceived risk, because consumers may perceive as "less risky" those products and services that make them "feel good." Accordingly, it is expected that there will be a negative relationship between positive emotions and perceived risk.

Dowling and Staelin (1994) also conceive of prior knowledge to consist of information concerning the attributes (quality, price, etc.) of the product, based on consumers' past experiences. They postulate that such perceived differences lead to perceived risk and, thus, a positive relationship is depicted between these constructs.

RESEARCH RESULTS

Purpose of the Study

To validate the model in Figure 7.1 in this chapter.

The Units of Observation

Products and services were used as the units of observation. This level of analysis is especially appropriate for the model discussed earlier, which specifies certain product types (hedonic and utilitarian) as the purely exogenous constructs in the model. Thirty users for each of 146 products and services were surveyed on all the variables of interest in the study, and the mean for the 30 responses was accepted as the aggregate "score" for each variable for a particular product. This was done for a total of 146 cases, and an aggregate data set was, thus, compiled in which products or services were the units of analysis.

Selection of the Sample

A sample of 150 products and services was randomly selected for analysis from the Standard Industrial Classification Manual (Statistical Policy Division 1987). Only commonly used consumer products and services were accepted into the sample. Table 7.1 lists the final 146 products and services in the study.

TABLE 7.1   Products and Services in the Study

botanical gardens	pillowcases	room air conditioners
embroidery kits	blankets	income tax prep service
sewing thread	amusement parks	laxatives
hair tonics	barbecue grills	frying pans
potato chips	museums	continuing education
blood donor stations	sports protectors	pocket knives
dance studios	time clocks	perfumes
electric fans	football equipment	cruise ships
brake repair service	ballpoint pens	flowers
auto battery service	bars	women's underwear
high schools	burglar alarms	lightbulbs
sunglasses	trucks	gasoline
frozen meat pies	service apparel	seeds and bulbs
bacon	baby strollers	swimming pools
condo associations	men's belts	air mattresses
children's wear	stuffed animals	windshield wipers
wedding dresses	house slippers	youth centers
lodging houses	cigarette lighters	suntan lotion
analgesics	motion picture theaters	child daycare
bath tubs	cottage cheese	computer games
laundry soap	domestic services	veterinary service
self-service laundry	doctors' offices	personal computers
greeting cards	cornflakes	mail order magazines
canned soft drinks	work gloves	record albums
atlases	canned seafood	candy
pianos	talcum powder	cotton towels
newspapers	smoking tobacco	tampons
locks	cooking ranges	razor blades
macaroni	telephone service	hair shampoo
sherbet/ices	encyclopedias	synthetic sweeteners
cameras	billiard and pool cues	women's handbags
ketchup	fever remedies	shopping centers
russian dressing	margarines	air passenger carriers
freeze-dried coffee	food trucks	boys'/men's slacks
granola bars	political organizations	universities
kitchen utensils	Christmas trees	golf equipment
flashlights	Halloween lanterns	classical music
refined salt	eyeglasses	nightclubs
office furniture	microwave ovens	carpets

TABLE 7.1   Products and Services in the Study—cont'd

women's slips	couches	bottled iced tea
novelty stores	potatoes	frozen french toast
chewing gum	cigarettes	women's negligees
ice cubes	guns	fitness salons
earthenware	household poisons	bingo parlors
household brushes	canned fruits	motor vehicle oil filters
cigars	beauticians	coats
zippers	medical laboratories	erasers
creamers	automotive tire dealers	hosiery
spices	vegetable cooking oil	

Procedure

A field survey of 30 actual users was conducted for each of the 146 products and services. None of the users were used for more than one product; thus, a total of 4,380 respondents (mean age = 32.2) were surveyed. A total of 11,139 approaches were made in 89 judgmentally determined locations in the northeastern United States, mostly in the states of Massachusetts, Connecticut, New York, and New Jersey.

Surveys were conducted, as much as possible, at places where the product/service was consumed or purchased in order to obtain the most immediate and direct feedback on their consumption experiences. Thus, for instance, the surveys for botanical gardens were conducted at the Beardsley Park Zoo, in Connecticut; embroidery kits and sewing thread at a craft and art supply store; hair tonics at a hairstyling salon; potato chips at a grocery store; blood donor stations at a Red Cross blood drive; dance studios at a dance studio; electric fans at the appliances section of a department store; and so forth. Where this was not possible (e.g., mail order magazines), surveys were conducted in a centralized location such as a shopping mall.

Measures

Emotion. In a study of emotion prototypes, Shaver et al. (1987) arrived at two superordinate constructs (positive and negative affect) and five basic emotion levels (joy, love, sadness, anger, and fear) that are underlying dimensions of positive and negative affect. Six emotion terms (three for positive emotion and three for negative emotion) were chosen for this study with an eye to their applicability towards the consumption of products and services.

Perceived differences between alternatives. The cognitive, ratiocinative aspect of information processing in the consumption experience was assessed by some common attributes of products and services, namely quality, value, convenience, efficiency, reliability, economy, dependability, and price.

Hedonic and utilitarian values. These variables were measured by six items on a seven-point agree/disagree scale. Hedonic was operationalized as: "This product is a luxury for me," "I love this product," and "I feel good when I use this product." Utilitarian was operationalized as "This product is a necessity for me," "I use this product frequently," and "I rely on this product."

Perceived risk. Perceived risk was operationalized by the following five items in a seven-point agree/disagree scale: "This product involves financial risk for me," "This product could perform poorly and let me down," "This product could cause me physical pain," "This product could cause me mental pain," and "Others could think badly of me because of this product."

Results

The model in Figure 7.1 was tested. Hedonic and utilitarian values were not significantly correlated and, thus, they represent orthogonal constructs. Hedonic had a significant positive relationship with all of the endogenous variables. Moreover, all of the relationships ranged from moderately strong (.31 with perceived differences and .17 with negative emotion) to very strong (.81 with positive emotion and .48 with perceived risk). Utilitarian was positively related to perceived differences (.31) and negatively related to positive emotion (–.17), but it was not significantly related to negative emotion. In general, these results support the view espoused by Holbrook and Hirschman (1982) that different types of products are capable of eliciting different types of rational and emotional responses.

There was no relationship between perceived differences among alternatives and perceived risk. However, both the emotion dimensions had significant relationships with perceived risk. The negative emotion dimension had a strong positive influence (.56) and the positive emotion dimension had a moderately strong negative influence (–.26) on perceived risk. It seems that products that are capable of eliciting undesirable feelings are also associated with greater perceived risk whereas products that potentially generate pleasant feelings are associated with less perceived risk. This is in keeping with the theoretical stand in this chapter that emotion represents a type of prior knowledge and that, accordingly, it should be related to perceived risk.

The finding the negative emotions create a threatening consumption situation for consumers and lead to perceptions of risk about the product or service holds important implications for managers in terms of brand loyalty and other phenomena that are affected by perceptions of risk. Thus, a brand that reduces perceived risk in a "high anxiety" product category should engender greater acceptance. (for instance, "Ultra Air" promotes itself as "the least annoying airline.") In fact, the marketing of products and services today increasingly attempts to alleviate consumers' feelings of depression, nervousness, and mistrust (Rickard, 1994) and the results of the present study justify this approach for a wide variety of products and services because these were found to be capable of arousing negative emotions and corresponding perceived risk.

Products and services that elicit positive emotions were negatively related to perceived risk in the study. It would appear that products and services that are capable of providing enjoyment are also associated with an accompanying sense of diminished risk concerning the consequences of such hedonic fulfillment. This is an important finding for public policy issues because it suggests that hedonic experiences with products such as cigarettes and alcoholic beverages may lead to lessened awareness of the risk associated with such products. This may provide one explanation for the finding that certain warning labels are ignored by consumers of alcoholic beverages (Barlow & Wogalter, 1993). In the area of retail sales, the same finding could lead to speculation that those retailers who create an entertaining retail environment could obtain higher than average prices for their products by alleviating perceived price risk through positive consumption experiences. In the area of promotions, the implication is straightforward. Advertisements for hedonic products, such as sports cars and ice cream, which emphasize the pleasure that can be derived from the use of the product (Chaudhuri, 1993; MacInnis & Stayman, 1993) may reduce consumers' consideration of, for instance, safety issues and overindulgence.

8[1]

TRUST AND COMMITMENT

"Trust me"

(Arnold Schwarzenegger in *Eraser*)

"This is really about trust. Who do you trust? . . . You can trust me. You can trust Jack Kemp. We're not going to promise you some pie-in-the-sky economic plan just to try to get you to vote for us, say, 'Well, we got their votes, we're now President and Vice President, let's go fishing.' Or whatever."

(Bob Dole as cited in the *New York Times*, August 28, 1996)

Brand names, whether those of movie stars, politicians, or automobiles, derive at least some part of their attraction from a promise of trust. Similarly, brand commitment (or brand loyalty) would appear, to some extent, to have affective foundations because it is not uncommon to hear people say that they "love" their new Honda Civic or their favorite flavor of Ben and Jerry's ice cream. Brand trust and brand affect have not, however, been widely considered as determinants of brand commitment in spite of the recent trend in marketing literature towards the notion of "relationship" marketing with its emphasis on commitment (Gundlach, Achrol, & Mentzer, 1995).

This chapter extends the study of relational exchanges to consumer markets using brands as the unit of analysis. I propose certain product class determinants (hedonic and importance aspects of product involvement, perceived risk in choosing between brands in the product category) as determinants of brand commitment and brand outcomes (market share, relative price). Brand trust and brand affect are also modeled as intervening variables in the process.

[1] Parts of this chapter are reprinted with permission from *Journal of Marketing*, published by the American Marketing Association, Chaudhuri, Arjun & Morris B. Holbrook, 2001, Vol. 65 (April), 81–93.

RELATIONSHIP MARKETING

Relationship marketing has been defined as "all marketing activities directed toward establishing, developing, and maintaining successful relational exchanges" (Morgan & Hunt, 1994, p. 22). Most empirical work to date in relationship marketing has been directed toward understanding the relational exchanges in business-to-business marketing, such as the relationships between users and providers of market research (Moorman, Zaltman, & Deshpande, 1992) and industrial buyers and sellers (Doney & Cannon, 1997), and the reasons underlying the strategic alliances between manufacturers and retailers of automotive tires (Morgan & Hunt, 1994). However, the topic of relationship marketing also lends itself to understanding the relationships that brands have with consumers. What, for instance, is the role of consumer trust and commitment in determining brand outcomes such as greater market share and relative price? Morgan and Hunt found that trust and commitment are key variables in buyer-seller relationships in the industrial market. The objective of this chapter is to determine whether trust and commitment are also key variables in the relationships that brands have with consumers in the consumer market. In addition, I look at a third key variable, brand affect, because this concept has emotional underpinnings that are appropriate for the consumer market.

It has also been suggested that relational exchanges in the consumer market involve effects such as the level of perceived risk in the product category (Sheth & Parvatiyar, 1995). Accordingly, I suggest that the constructs of brand trust, brand affect, brand commitment, and brand outcomes have specific product class determinants such as the hedonic and importance aspects of product involvement and the extent of perceived risk in choosing between brands (henceforth referred to as "brand choice risk"). This should be of great interest to brand managers and others who are more concerned with decisions that relate to brands than with individual level differences.

MODEL

Figure 8.1 suggests that brand-level constructs such as brand trust, brand affect, and brand commitment (both attitudinal and purchase commitment) are derived from product class determinants such as hedonic and importance aspects of product involvement and brand choice risk. Van Trijp, Hoyer, and Inman (1996) found that similar product category variables affected variety-seeking behavior, and I attempt to understand whether this applies to a related concept in consumer behavior, namely brand commitment. Further, I try to examine the process by which brand commitment may be related to product class effects.

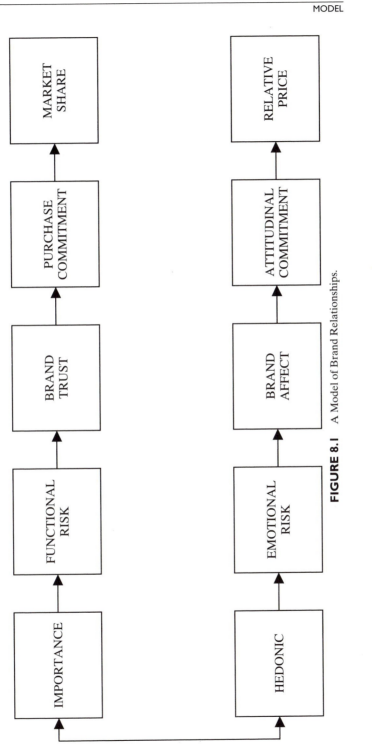

FIGURE 8.1 A Model of Brand Relationships.

PRODUCT INVOLVEMENT

Product involvement has generally been considered to be "the relevance of the product to the needs and values of the consumer" (Zaichkowsky, 1985, p. 342). Although there may be other ways in which a product may be relevant to a consumer, two aspects have been clearly identified and agreed upon in the involvement literature—the importance aspect and the hedonic aspect (Laurent & Kapferer, 1985; McQuarrie & Munson, 1987; Zaichkowsky, 1985, 1987, 1994). These aspects also correspond to the archetypal constructs of emotion and reason with which people process information about their environment. Indeed, the marketing literature has previously identified "affective" and "cognitive" types of involvement (Park & Young, 1986) and it has been observed that consumers assign both emotional and rational values to products (Zaichkowsky, 1987).

Product Involvement and Brand Commitment

What is the relationship between the two dimensions of product involvement in a product category and brand commitment? Is brand commitment higher for important and hedonic products like automobiles and personal computers than for products like toilet tissue and chewing gum? There is very little evidence on the subject in spite of the obvious managerial implications in understanding the theoretical underpinnings of brand commitment. Understanding, for instance, that brand commitment may be more prevalent in high involvement product classes would suggest that brand managers in high involvement products should spend more on advertising and other brand loyalty enhancement strategies whereas brands in low involvement product categories should allocate more funds to sales promotion and similar strategies that encourage loyalty to price and not to the brand.

The skeletal evidence that does exist on the topic appears to be inconclusive. In a study of product involvement and brand commitment (similar to brand loyalty), Traylor (1981) examined 12 product categories among 40 consumer households and found that results varied among product categories. He concluded that ". . . a positive relationship appears to be a product specific phenomenon rather than the general rule suggested in the literature. At the very least, the relationship between product involvement and brand commitment is an ambiguous one" (p. 55). Traylor also came to the conclusion that ". . . in highly ego-involving product-purchase decisions, many criteria come into play, only one of which may be the brand" (p. 54).

It appears that other factors may also be involved in understanding the relationship between brand commitment and product involvement. Four such additional constructs are included in the model in Figure 8.1. These are constructs of perceived risk (both functional and emotional elements, as discussed below) in the product category and brand trust and brand affect.

BRAND CHOICE RISK

In Chapter 7 I dealt with perceived risk in terms of the overall risk perceived by consumers in the product category. This type of risk in the product category is also referred to as inherent or latent risk and is different from the risk in choosing between brands in the product category or brand choice risk. For instance, Bettman (1973) distinguished between two types of risk: "Inherent risk is the latent risk a product class holds for a consumer—the innate degree of conflict the product class is able to arouse. Handled risk is the amount of conflict the product class is able to arouse when the buyer chooses a brand from a product class in his usual buying situation" (p. 184). It is the latter type of risk (risk in choosing between brands in the product class) that I conceptualize in this chapter as a consequence of product involvement and a determinant of brand trust and brand affect. I call this *brand choice risk*, and I suggest that the five types of brand choice risk identified in the literature—financial, social, psychological, physical, and performance (Jacoby & Kaplan, 1972; Murphy & Enis, 1986)—group into two predominant types of brand choice risk, functional (financial, physical, and performance risk) and emotional (social and psychological risk).

The model in Figure 8.1 postulates that brand trust, brand affect, and also functional and emotional brand choice risk are intervening variables in the relationship of product involvement to brand commitment. In other words, brand trust, brand affect, and the two types of brand choice risk are the links between product involvement and product commitment. These constructs explain why product involvement may be related to brand commitment. Products that are high in involvement (both importance and hedonic dimensions) are also perceived to present greater risk in terms of brand choice in the product category. Greater perceptions of risk in choosing between brands in the product category, in turn, lead to greater trust and affect toward a particular brand that is relied upon. Television sets, for example, are high in both importance and hedonic involvement (Laurent & Kapferer, 1985). This may motivate consumers to process information about brands resulting in knowledge about differences between brands of television sets. Such knowledge about significant differences among brands in the product category may generate perceptions of high risk in choosing the wrong brand of television. As a result, consumers restrict their brand choices to a single trusted brand, say Sony. This mediated model of the effects of product class variables on brand commitment is presented here as a fuller, more complete depiction of the process of brand commitment.

Brand Choice Risk and Product Involvement

In the model in Figure 8.1 I suggest two explanations of the relationship between involvement and commitment. First, product involvement with an important product category leads to higher perceptions of functional risk in choosing between brands in the product category and this, in turn, leads to greater commitment to a particular brand as a result of greater trust toward that favorite brand.

Consider, for instance, a diner who patronizes only one restaurant. One explanation of this behavior could involve a low level of product importance with restaurants, a lack of knowledge of other restaurants, and, thus, the consumer is habituated to a single place of patronage. Another, perhaps more likely, explanation is that the consumer is highly involved, has visited other restaurants; realizes that all restaurants are not the same in terms of quality, reliability, and the like; perceives risk in trying new and varied restaurants in terms of taste and physical safety of the food; has discovered a particular restaurant that can be trusted and relied upon in terms of the quality and safety of its food; and now chooses to frequent this restaurant more so than other less trustworthy places. Moreover, as a result of brand trust, this committed consumer may even increase his or her usual frequency of eating out every week (instead of cooking at home), thus providing the favorite restaurant with increases in sales volume and market share. He or she may now also find "other uses" for the brand such as take out when in a hurry, encouraging group visits with friends to this "favorite" restaurant, asking the restaurant to cater a party, and so on. All this will generate additional sales and consequent brand outcomes such as greater market share for the restaurant. These outcomes result from greater brand trust and brand commitment in an important product category where consumers perceive significant functional risk in choosing an unfamiliar or "wrong" brand.

Another scenario is that the consumer sees significant brand choice risk in terms of the emotional (social and psychological) consequences of using the "wrong" brand in a highly hedonic product category. For instance, a well-known advertisement by clothing manufacturer Hart, Schaffner, & Marx declared that "the wrong suit could certainly slow you down" from reaching the top of the corporate ladder, and then presented the advertised brand as the "right suit." Advertising messages of this nature incorporate emotional brand choice risk. These social and psychological dimensions of risk, in particular, may be especially high for hedonic products in which the potential for both pleasure and pain is high, as discussed earlier in Chapter 7.

Perceptions of the consequences of choosing the wrong brand may be heightened for products with a high potential for pleasure (hedonic involvement) relative to more mundane products that are used on a regular basis. These are not "everyday" products but products that are occasionally used and, thus, cherished more by most consumers. Such products may be high not only in their pleasure potential, but also in their "pain" potential in terms of the social and psychological dangers present in choosing the wrong brand. Thus, highly pleasurable items (say, designer clothing) can have undesirable consequences in their aftermath, and choosing the right brand is important from an emotional risk point of view. Similarly, perfumes, fashionwear, candy, and alcohol not only may provide a great deal of pleasure but also have the potential for undesirable social and psychological consequences. Finally, such products may be closely associated with the consumer's self-concept and social identity and perceived differences in quality between brands may translate into greater risk regarding the social and psychological consequences of choosing the wrong brand. Overall, the pleasure potential in the product enhances perceptions of risk in the buying process because a stimulus that has greater motivational potential (i.e., pleasure) leads to greater appraisal and evaluation.

In sum, the emotional dimension of brand choice risk and hedonic involvement are expected to be positively related. I submit here that the potential for pleasure in the product class is a basic motivational force governing consumer purchasing and, further, that it motivates a heightened level of processing of the subsequent level of emotional risk in choosing between brands in the product class.

Brand Choice Risk, Brand Trust, and Brand Affect

I propose that emotional and functional elements of brand choice risk will have different effects on brand trust and brand affect. More specifically, functional brand choice risk will be positively related to brand trust and emotional brand choice risk will be positively related to brand affect. If the functional elements of risk are high in the product class, it is expected that consumers will attribute greater trust to a certain brand in the product class. Similarly, when the emotional elements of risk are high in a product class, it is expected that consumers will derive more affect from a particular brand in the product class. Brand affect is defined as "the potential in a brand to elicit a positive emotional response in the average consumer as a result of its use."

In consonance with the definition of trust provided by Moorman, Zaltman, and Deshpande (1992, p. 315), I define brand trust as "the willingness of the average consumer to rely on the ability of the brand to perform its stated function." Other definitions of trust also emphasize the notion of reliance as crucial to trust (Morgan & Hunt, 1994, p. 23). Moorman, Zaltman, and Deshpande, and Doney and Cannon (1997) also stress that the notion of trust is relevant only in situations of uncertainty. Trust reduces the risk and uncertainty in an environment in which the consumer feels especially vulnerable because the consumer knows that the trusted brand can be relied upon. This is in accordance with our earlier claim that brand trust will be higher in cases where the product class has high levels of brand choice risk. In particular, brand trust is expected to increase when the functional elements of risk are high (i.e., when the ability of other brands to perform their tasks is questionable and dubious). The literature on trust in marketing appears to suggest that the construct involves a "calculative process" (Doney & Cannon, p. 37) involving the ability of the other party (in this case, the brand) to continue to meet its obligations and also each partner's estimation of the costs and rewards of staying in the relationship. Accordingly, I suggest that brand trust will be positively related to the more ratiocinative, analytical, functional dimension of brand choice risk whereas brand affect will result when the emotional consequences of choosing the wrong brand are high. Overall, I view brand trust as involving a process that is well thought out and well considered whereas the development of brand affect is a more spontaneous, immediate, and less cognitive process. Sheth and Parvatiyar (1995) also consider social risk separately as a determinant of relational exchanges. High levels of uncertainty in the social and psychological appropriateness of other brands in the product class are likely to raise the level of emotional bonding with the present brand of choice. This leads me to propose that (a) brand trust increases as functional brand choice risk increases and (b) brand affect increases as emotional brand choice risk increases.

EFFECTS OF BRAND TRUST AND BRAND AFFECT ON BRAND COMMITMENT

The emotional and rational elements in the model come together in the final relational construct of brand commitment. According to Morgan and Hunt (1994), trust and commitment are key relational variables because they encourage the respective partners in the relationship to (a) work at preserving the relationship, (b) avoid alternative relations with other partners, and (c) reduce the perception of risk in the environment. Gundlach, Achrol, and Mentzer (1995) warn that these relational constructs can be very complex and overlapping, but they view commitment as essential to a long-term successful relationship. Commitment reduces uncertainty and the cost of seeking and incurring new relational exchanges.

Brand trust leads to brand commitment because trust creates exchange relationships that are highly valued (Morgan & Hunt, 1994) or important. In fact, commitment has been defined as "an enduring desire to maintain a valued relationship" (Moorman, Zaltman, & Deshpande, 1992, p. 316). Thus, commitment is part of the ongoing process of continuing and maintaining a valuable and important relationship that has been created by trust. In other words, trust and commitment should be related because trust is important in relational exchanges and commitment is also reserved for such important and valued relationships.

Further, brand commitment entails vulnerability in the sense that consumers now forsake all other alternatives and rely on a single brand that they expect will not let them down. Thus, only trustworthy partnerships lead to committed relationships because such partnerships are perceived to be less risky and more reliable. Further, Moorman, Zaltman, and Deshpande (1992) and Morgan and Hunt (1994) both found that trust leads to commitment in relational exchanges. In fact, the coefficient between trust and commitment was .53 in the study by Morgan and Hunt. Thus, in brand relationships as well, I suggest that brand commitment will increase as brand trust increases.

The emotional determinants of brand commitment need to be considered separately in the context of the maintenance of brand relationships. Gundlach, Achrol, and Mentzer (1995) suggest that commitment is associated with positive affect and that although this may prevent the exploration of other alternatives in the short-term, steady benefits in the long-term are likely to accrue from this "irrational" bonding. In particular, such a relationship or "affective attachment" (p. 79) is viewed to be the most beneficial in uncertain environments. Our notion of the relationship between brand affect and brand commitment is further predicated on the ties between positive emotional feelings and close relationships drawn from the literature on interpersonal relationships.

> The landscape of close human relationships presents so vivid a panorama of human evolution that the very phrase "close relationship" carries the implication of passions spent or anticipated, of feelings of every size, shape, and description of, at the very least, some experience of affect—an antiseptic term, but one that encompasses without prejudice the entire range of quality and intensity of human emotion and feeling. . . . Many do not consider a relationship between two people to be "close" unless there are strong positive affective ties between the participants. (Berscheid, 1983, p. 110)

Berscheid (1983) isolated two critical aspects of a close emotional relationship: the magnitude of the affect (or affective intensity) and the hedonic sign of the affect (positive/negative). I suggest that the close relationship of a brand with its consumers can also be predicted based on the level of positive affect generated by the brand. Strong and positive affective responses will be associated with high levels of brand commitment. In this connection, Dick and Basu (1994) also proposed that brand loyalty, similar to brand commitment, would be greater under conditions of greater positive emotional mood or affect. Thus, brands that make consumers "happy" should be associated with greater commitment. Although feelings of happiness and joy may not be prevalent in supplier-buyer relationships, I submit that positive emotional feelings such as happiness are very much a part of the relationship that brands have with consumers, that is, brand commitment will increase as brand affect increases.

Brand Commitment

At this juncture, I distinguish between this notion of brand commitment and the related concept of brand loyalty. Although brand loyalty has been recognized as possessing both dimensions of behavioral (or "spurious") and attitudinal (or "true") loyalty, the marketing literature has mainly emphasized only the behavioral dimension of the concept. Most often, researchers have measured brand loyalty according to the past purchasing patterns of consumers. However, as mentioned, it has been suggested that brand loyalty includes some degree of commitment toward the quality of the brand (Aaker, 1991; Assael, 1998; Beatty & Kahle, 1988; Jacoby & Chestnut, 1978), which is a function of both positive attitudes toward the brand and repetitive purchases. Accordingly, I consider brand commitment to occur when both brand purchasing intentions and attitudinal commitment for the brand are present. In keeping with Gundlach, Achrol, and Mentzer (1995), who extensively review the literature on commitment, brand commitment is defined as an average consumer's long-term, behavioral, and attitudinal disposition towards a relational brand. This is, of course, very similar to the classic definition by Jacoby and Chestnut (pp. 80–81) of brand loyalty as a function of both behavioral and psychological (attitudinal) processes. However, because brand loyalty is usually considered to be an individual-level variable, I have used the term *brand commitment* in this study, which is at the aggregate level of brands and not at the individual level.

Thus, the notion of brand commitment includes behavioral (purchase intent) and attitudinal brand loyalty and should obtain the same brand outcomes as have always been predicted for brands with a high level of loyalty. Indeed, brand loyalty is a concept whose importance has been recognized in the marketing literature for many years. Howard and Sheth (1969) pointed out that greater brand loyalty among consumers leads to greater sales of the brand (p. 132). Aaker (1991) discussed the role of brand loyalty in the brand equity process, and he specifically noted that brand loyalty leads to certain marketing advantages such as reduced marketing costs, more new customers, and greater trade leverage. Additionally, Dick and Basu (1994) suggested other marketing advantages as a result of brand loyalty such as favorable word of mouth and greater resistance among loyal consumers to competitive strategies. Brand outcomes such as market share and relative price, in turn, have been found to relate to profitability (Porter, 1980) and brand equity (Park & Srinivasan, 1994) and are, thus, worthwhile dependent variables for a study using brands as the units of analysis (see also Smith & Park, 1992).

In consonance with the past literature on brand loyalty, Figure 8.1 suggests that the consumer-level variables of brand trust, brand affect, and brand commitment (purchase and attitudinal components) are related to brand outcomes at the market level such as market share and relative price. Market share is defined as the sales of a brand expressed as a percentage of the total sales of all brands in the product class. It is expected that brands high in purchase commitment will also be high in market share due to higher levels of repeat purchases by the brand's users. This is predicated on the theory of double jeopardy described in the following section.

Purchase Commitment and Market Share

The theory of "double jeopardy" (Ehrenberg, Goodhart, & Baswise, 1990; McPhee, 1963), has advanced as one of the few "lawlike" generalizations in marketing (Ehrenberg et al. [1990], p. 90). Indeed, there is a considerable body of evidence that supports this theory (see Donthu, 1994; Ehrenberg et al. [1990] Fader & Schmittlein, 1993). The theory specifies that small market share brands are at a disadvantage, relative to large market share brands, in two ways. First, they have fewer buyers, and second, they are purchased less frequently by these few buyers. In contrast, more popular brands (or brands with large market share) have more buyers and they are also purchased more often by these many buyers. The principal reasons that have been advanced for the double jeopardy phenomenon are greater awareness and distribution support for high market share brands. For example, a high market share brand may be the only brand that is carried by some stores and, thus, distribution patterns may favor the habitual buying of high market share brands (Fader & Schmittlein, 1993).

Thus, brands with greater market share demonstrate greater levels of repeat purchasing behavior (purchase commitment in this study) among their buyers. In fact, the correlation between market share and number of purchases per buyer is around .6 for frequently purchased products (Ehrenberg et al., 1990, p. 83). Accordingly, I can expect that in this study as well, there will be a positive relationship between a brand's market share and its purchase commitment among its buyers.

Attitudinal Commitment and Relative Price

Relative price is defined as "the price of a brand relative to the price of its leading competitor." It is also posited that brands high in attitudinal commitment also will be high in relative price. This is predicated on the theory of brand equity.

Brand equity has been described by the Marketing Science Institute as "the set of associations and behavior on the part of a brand's customers, channel members, and parent corporation that permits the brand to earn greater volume or greater margins than it could without the brand name" (Leuthesser, 1988). Winters (1991) and Aaker (1996) both reviewed different ways of assessing brand equity, and both authors came to the conclusion that the price of a brand in the marketplace was a critical indicator of the brand's equity. Thus, because attitudinal commitment constitutes the overall evaluation of a brand at the consumer level, it should be positively related to the overall evaluation of the brand (its brand equity as represented by its price) at the market level. Further, Bello and Holbrook (1995) define brand equity as the price premium that the associations of a brand name contribute to the brand's price. The definition of brand equity by the Marketing Science Institute provided earlier also defines brand equity as the set of consumer associations about the brand that lead to greater margins for the brand. Finally, to cite Keller (1993), "Consumers with a strong, favorable brand attitude should be more willing to pay premium prices for the brand" (p. 9). Thus, based on the past literature on brand equity, it is expected that there will be a significant and positive relationship between a brand's attitudinal commitment and its price.

Aaker (1991) states that brand equity "assets" (such as brand attitudes, loyalty, and commitment) could produce price premiums and other brand equity outcomes for the brand. Indeed, there appears to be sufficient justification to expect a relationship between brand commitment and brand equity outcomes such as market share and premium prices. If we view brand equity outcomes (market share, relative price) as "the profit potential of a brand," then there are basically three outcomes by way of which such profits might accrue—lower costs, greater sales, and higher prices. Consider that these three outcomes are also the result of manifest brand commitment toward a brand. First, brand-loyal users are willing to search for their favorite brand (Cunningham, 1967) and they require less advertising frequency, resulting in lower costs for advertising and distribution (Aaker, 1991). Second, brand commitment leads to greater and continual sales because the same brand is repeatedly purchased, irrespective of situational constraints (Assael, 1998). Also, consumers may use more of the brand to which they are loyal, because they may "like" using the brand or because they identify with the image of the brand (Upshaw, 1995). Finally, committed consumers are willing to pay more for a brand because they perceive some unique value in the brand that no other alternative can provide (Jacoby & Chestnut, 1978; Pessemier, 1959). Price premiums have also recently been closely associated with the notions of brand loyalty and brand equity (Aaker, 1996; Bello & Holbrook, 1995; Park & Srinivasan, 1994; Winters, 1991).

In sum, it is expected that there will be a significant and positive relationship between a brand's purchase commitment and its market share and between a brand's attitudinal commitment and its relative price in the marketplace.

RESEARCH RESULTS

Purpose of the Study

To validate the model in Figure 8.1 in this chapter.

Method

The aggregate-level data for the study was compiled from four separate consumer surveys conducted in four phases. Collecting the responses separately for almost every level of the model ensures that the linkages between the dependent and independent variables are not artifacts of asking the same respondents to provide both sets of answers in a single questionnaire. The use of four separate examples removes this kind of response bias and provides a stronger test of the relationships of interest. The aggregate-level data generated during each phase were merged together to form a single data set for the study.

Phase One

Data Collection

The data collection procedures in the first phase were the same as the procedures described in Chapter 7 for the sample of 146 products. These are not repeated here.

Measures

Hedonic and Importance Measures. McQuarrie and Munson's (1987) 14-item semantic differential scale (see Appendix I at the end of the chapter), which has three subscales, was utilized to measure product involvement in the study. The "risk" subscale was not used because of its obviousy tautological connections with brand choice risk.

Phase Two

Data Collection

In Phase Two, the two types of brand choice risk were measured by a phone survey of 30 respondents for each product category. Once again, an aggregate level of analysis was used, this time with 89 of the sample of 146 products and services from Phase One selected for inclusion. The telephone survey in Phase Two sampled 2,670 respondents (mean age = 42.6). To reach these users, 7,729 total phone approaches were randomly made from 61 different phone directories in the northeastern U.S.—again, mostly from Massachusetts, Connecticut, New York, and New Jersey.

Measures

Functional and Emotional Brand Choice Risk. The scale by Jacoby and Kaplan (1972) was used to measure functional and emotional brand choice risk. The scale deals with five components of brand choice risk, financial, performance, physical, psychological, and social. Appendix II provides the five items used in the questionnaire.

Phase Three

Data Collection

Forty-five of the original 146 products were included in Phase Three by virtue of having easily identifiable branded alternatives and representing commonly used consumer products for which it would be feasible to locate

30 users of a brand in Phase Four. Questionnaires were mailed to product managers of 328 brands in the 45 product categories. One hundred forty-nine completed surveys were obtained for a response rate of 45%. A list of all 45 product categories in the final data set appears in Table 8.1.

In general, Table 8.1 reveals a wide representation of brands drawn from a variety of consumer products and industries.

Measures

Market Share, Relative Price. These measures in Phase Three were obtained from the information provided by the product managers in the questionnaire. Specifically, these product managers were asked to define the served market of the brand and to answer a series of questions on their brand, keeping this served market in mind. For instance, market share was measured by asking

TABLE 8.1 Products in the Study

1.	analgesics	24.	kitchen utensils
2.	automotive tires	25.	laundry soap
3.	bacon	26.	light bulbs
4.	ballpoint pens	27.	macaroni
5.	barbecue grills	28.	margarines
6.	bottled iced tea	29.	mattresses
7.	boys'/men's slacks	30.	men's underwear
8.	cameras	31.	microwave ovens
9.	candy	32.	pantyhose
10.	canned fruits	33.	perfumes
11.	canned soft drinks	34.	personal computers
12.	cereals	35.	potato chips
13.	chewing gum	36.	razor blades
14.	children's wear	37.	room air conditioners
15.	coffee	38.	salad dressing
16.	cooking ranges	39.	shampoos
17.	cottage cheese	40.	suntan lotion
18.	electric fans	41.	synthetic sweeteners
19.	flashlights	42.	trucks
20.	gasoline	43.	vegetable cooking oil
21.	golf clubs	44.	women's handbags
22.	hair tonics	45.	women's underwear
23.	ice cream		

Note: There were three brands for each product in the final data set, except for bottled iced tea and canned soft drinks, which had four brands each. Thus, the final data set contained 137 brands.

respondents directly for the brand's market share within its served market. Relative price was measured by dividing the brand's price by the price of the brand that was the market leader. If the brand itself was the market leader, then its price was divided by the price of the next leading brand.

Phase Four

Data Collection

Interviews to collect data on brand trust, brand affect, and brand commitment were conducted. Data were obtained for 137 brands from 4,110 respondents (mean age = 35.8). To obtain this sample, a total of 12,542 approaches were made in Connecticut, Massachusetts, New Jersey, and New York. Surveys were conducted mostly in shopping centers and malls. The means, typically based on 30 responses per brand (with some exceptions due to missing data), were calculated for each item on the survey, resulting in a data set with 137 brands as the units of observation.

Measures

Brand Trust, Brand Affect, Brand Commitment. Brand trust was measured as a three-item index based on seven-point ratings of agreement (1 = very strongly disagree; 9 = very strongly agree) with the following three statements: "I trust this brand"; "I rely on this brand"; and "This brand is safe." Brand affect was measured by the sum of three similarly rated items: "I feel good when I use this brand"; "This brand makes me happy"; and "This brand gives me pleasure." Purchase brand commitment was measured by agreement with the following two statements: "I will buy this brand the next time I buy [product name]" and "I intend to keep purchasing this brand." Attitudinal brand commitment was measured by the statements "I am committed to this brand" and "I would be willing to pay a higher price for this brand over other brands."

Final Data Set

In order to construct the final data set, the consumer-survey data set (Phase Four), based on the means of the 30 responses for each brand, was merged with the managerial-survey data set (Phase Three) for the corresponding brands. Next, the product-class data (Phases One and Two) on perceived differences among alternatives, hedonic and utilitarian value, and brand choice risk were entered for each brand in the data set. This resulted in a data set of 137 brands.

Results

The model in Figure 8.1 was tested. Hedonic and importance values were significantly correlated together (r = .44; p < .05). Hedonic had a significant, strong, and positive relationship with emotional risk (.43) and with brand affect (.40). Hedonic was also significantly related to purchase commitment, but it was a negative relationship (–.30). Importance was strongly related to functional risk (.41) and moderately related to brand trust (.21). In general, these results support the view that the two different types of product involvement are capable of eliciting different types of brand choice risk and, consequently, either brand trust or brand affect. As expected, importance was not related to either brand affect or emotional risk and hedonic was not related to either brand trust or functional risk.

However, both brand trust and brand affect had significant relationships with the two types of brand commitment. Brand trust had a strong positive influence (.34) on purchase commitment and also on attitudinal commitment (.34). Brand affect also had a strong positive effect on purchase commitment (.46) and on attitudinal commitment (.33). However, only purchase commitment was related to market share (.25) and only attitudinal commitment was related to relative price (.22). This is in keeping with the expectation that the two types of brand commitment lead to two different types of brand outcomes. The results of the study indicate that there are two routes to brand outcomes—one rational and the other emotional. The former begins with the importance dimension of product involvement that translates into functional risk, greater trust in a particular brand, greater repurchase commitment, and greater market share for the brand. The latter originates in the pleasure potential inherent in the product (hedonic) and leads to knowledge of emotional risk and subsequent greater brand affect, greater attitudinal commitment, and higher relative price in the marketplace. Both brand trust and affect lead to greater brand commitment, but they have very different product class antecedents and very different brand outcomes.

Almost all conceptualizations of brand equity agree today that the phenomenon involves the value added to a product by consumers' associations and perceptions of a particular brand name (Aaker, 1991; Baldinger, 1990; Keller, 1993; Winters, 1991). Thus, there are two aspects of brand equity—one from the point of view of the firm and the other from that of the consumer. The firm/trade aspect of brand equity appears to be built around brand outcomes such as relative price and market share, whereas "customer-based brand equity" (Keller, p. 1) appears to have consumer associations of the brand at its core. However, the role that brand trust and brand affect play in the relationship of brand associations, such as brand commitment, to brand equity outcomes has not been explicitly considered in the literature. It is suggested in this research that brand trust and brand affect are separate constructs from brand commitment and that they play a crucial role in the relationship of customer-based brand equity to brand equity outcomes such as market share and relative price.

This conceptualization is corroborated in the empirical results of the present study in which very different outcomes were evidenced for brand trust and brand affect on the one hand, and brand commitment on the other. Although brand trust and brand affect were both positively related to brand commitment, they were not significantly related to either market share or relative price. Brand commitment, however, was significantly related to both market share and relative price. Attitudinal commitment was positively related to relative price and purchase commitment was related to market share. In sum, the different types of brand commitment may be considered to be the link between brand trust and brand affect and different types of market-based brand equity outcomes.

In general, then, the study finds two clear pathways to brand outcomes. One that is guided by a rational, thoughtful, deliberative process and another that is emotional, more instinctive, and spontaneous. The "emotional" path represented by hedonic, emotional risk, brand affect, and attitudinal commitment leads to relative price as the brand outcome. The "rational" path represented by importance, functional risk, brand trust, and purchase commitment leads to market share. Emotional and rational processing in consumers' minds can have very different brand outcomes in the marketplace.

Implications

Marketing managers can use these results to justify expenditures on promotions that create long-term effects (such as brand commitment, trust, and affect) on consumers because the consumer-level constructs are related to profitable brand outcomes. Moreover, if we are able to better relate both the consumer and market levels on which brands perform, then our overall understanding of the antecedents of brand outcomes is enhanced, leading to improved marketing mix strategies. For instance, brand communication strategies may be derived with special regard to the product class determinants of brand outcomes; one such implication for advertising was made earlier. For products high in hedonic involvement, ads should demonstrate that all brands are not the same in the product class *and* also show the emotional consequences of choosing the "wrong" brand in the product category and the positive brand affect from choosing the "right" brand. For products low in hedonic value but high in importance value, ads should demonstrate the functional elements of risk in the product class and emphasize trust in the advertised brand. Considerations of product safety, performance standards, and related financial loss become more important for these products because they lack the inherent motivational potential to produce pleasure. In either case, the notion of brand choice risk and the two dimensions of product involvement are clearly relevant.

APPENDIX I

Product Involvement

McQuarrie and Munson's (1987) 14-item semantic differential scale was used to measure the importance and hedonic aspects of product involvement.

irrelevant—:—:—:—:—:—:—relevant[a]
fun—:—:—:—:—:—:—not fun[b]
important—:—:—:—:—:—:—unimportant[a]
interesting—:—:—:—:—:—:—uninteresting[b]
of no concern to me—:—:—:—:—:—:—of concern to me[a]
unexciting—:—:—:—:—:—:—exciting[b]
easy to go wrong—:—:—:—:—:—:—hard to go wrong[c]
matters to me—:—:—:—:—:—:—doesn't matter to me[a]
appealing—:—:—:—:—:—:—unappealing[b]
no risk—:—:—:—:—:—:—risky[c]
means nothing to me—:—:—:—:—:—:—means a lot to me[a]
says something about me—:—:—:—:—:—:— says nothing about me[b]
easy to choose—:—:—:—:—:—:—hard to pick[c]
tells me about a person—:—:—:—:—:—:—shows nothing[b]

[a] importance subscale
[b] hedonic subscale
[c] risk subscale (not used in the study)

APPENDIX II

Brand Choice Risk

These questions were taken from Jacoby and Kaplan's (1972) scale and presented to subjects in a nine-point scale anchored from "very low chances" to "very high chances."

1. What are the chances that you stand to lose money if you try an unfamiliar brand of ——————, either because it won't work at all or because it costs more than it should to keep it in good shape?
2. What are the chances that there will be something wrong with an unfamiliar brand of —————— or that it will not work properly?
3. What are the chances that an unfamiliar brand of —————— may not be safe; that is, it may be harmful or injurious to your health?
4. What are the chances that an unfamiliar brand of —————— will not fit in well with your self-image or self-concept or the way you think about yourself?
5. What are the chances that an unfamiliar brand of —————— will affect the way others think of you?

9[1]

VALUE

"How many of your satisfied customers will remain if your competition offered them better value?"

(Bradley Gale, Marketing Science Conference, 1999)

This chapter extends the study of customer value to retail markets. I propose two types of customer value in a retail environment—merchandise value and differentiation value. I also propose a model that describes two routes from these two types of value leading to different outcomes. First, merchandise value leads to satisfaction, repatronage intent, and customer share. This route, based on cognitions of what is received versus what is sacrificed, is utilitarian in nature and derives from a rational approach to shopping. Second, differentiation value leads to positive affect, commitment, and willingness to pay. This second route, based on store differentiation and uniqueness, is affective in nature and derives from a hedonic approach to shopping. Separate outcomes are envisaged for the two routes based on previous research.

Managers have increasingly begun to discuss the notion of customer value as an alternative to the satisfaction paradigm. For instance, Reichheld (1996) describes how, of those customers reporting satisfaction, more than 85% will switch in the next purchase cycle and how, of the 85%–90% of automobile purchasers who report high levels of satisfaction, only 40% will repurchase the same make or model. Thus, satisfaction is no longer enough in explaining consumer choices. In fact, it has also been suggested that value is what the customer really wants and that satisfaction is only the "report card" on how well a company is doing in delivering that value (Woodruff & Gardial, 1996).

Most theoretical work to date in customer value has focused on understanding the application of value in product settings, especially with regard to identifying the antecedents and consequences of value. Such conceptualizations usually adopt a quality-price, benefits versus costs, give-up versus

---

[1] This chapter is based on work in progress with Mark S. Ligas.

get-back orientation to customer value (Gale, 1994; Kotler & Armstrong, 2004; Zeithaml, 1988). Regarding retail markets, prior research (Baker, Parasuraman, Grewal, & Voss, 2002) has focused mostly on merchandise value, which also uses the "give-get" notion of value that is currently prevalent in the literature. In other words, a low-priced store offering high-quality merchandise would provide the greatest value for the customer.

This would appear, to some extent, to be borne out by reports in the popular press about the resurgence of retailers such as J.C. Penney who are focusing on delivering greater value for the money to their customers (Daniels, 2003). However, as also documented in the business media, offering quality merchandise at a lower price, as in the case of the Old Navy chain of stores, may not always lead to preferred outcomes in retailing because this may cannibalize the high margin sales of a sibling store such as Gap (Lee, 2003). Note also, that in spite of deep discounting in retail stores by Kohl's, Gap, and others, retail profits are expected to be significantly lower (Forest, 2003). Thus, providing consumers with greater merchandise value may not always be a profitable retail strategy. On the other hand there appears to be a consumer trend, exemplified by stores like Starbucks, for unique and special experiences in products and stores (Barrett, 2003). Companies like Starbucks also charge higher prices for such special experiences (Holmes, 2003).

Thus, there would appear to be at least two different routes to greater profitability that retailers are presently using in their marketing strategies and, in fact, have always used. The first is based on greater "value for money" for customers leading to greater sales and revenue for the company. This is a cost-based approach in which profits will accrue if the company can keep its costs under the low price floor set by its "value" pricing strategies. In addition to describing this strategy, Day and Wensley (1988) also suggest a "differentiated strategy." Under this differentiated framework, a company offers some value-added attribute, tangible or nontangible, which the customer perceives as superior, even unique, and for which the customer is willing to pay a premium price. This leads to greater profitability through greater revenue, because revenue is a function of both sales and price outcomes. In the context of retailing, I will refer to these two types of value as merchandise value and differentiation value.

The purpose of this chapter is to understand these two different sources of value (one rational, the other emotional) that consumers have with their retail stores. Further, I also consider the different consequences generated by these sources of value, and I arrive at separate outcomes such as satisfaction and repatronage intentions for merchandise value and affect and commitment for differentiation value. Consumer affect generated by the store environment has been viewed as a necessary factor for the development of commitment toward the store (Bitner, 1992; Hui & Bateson, 1991) and satisfaction frequently has been associated with purchase intent (Bolton, 1998). I further suggest that purchase intent leads to greater customer share or share-of-wallet, and that commitment leads to greater willingness to pay, as evidenced in recent research (Chaudhuri & Ray, 2003). Accordingly, I present in this chapter a comprehensive model of customer value in the retail environment.

PERSPECTIVES ON VALUE

The notion of value has a long and distinguished history in economics, starting with the work of Sir John Hicks (1939, 1973) and leading on to present work on valuation in economics, finance, and consumer behavior (Brendl, Markman, & Messner, 2003). Hicks conceived of capital as both an input and an output. To Hicks, the measurement of capital as output was value and it was "roughly equivalent to a capitalization of future net output for a given rate of return" (Hamouda, 1993, p. 151). Thus, in the retail context, we can also broadly view the notion of "value" as the capital available to the retailer in terms of the goods that it possesses and the present value of the future income streams that these goods will produce. Further, we can conceive of these goods as having both tangible and nontangible (brand names, in-store services provided, etc.) elements, both of which either independently or together represent the "quality" of the goods. And, we can conceive of certain outcomes accruing to the retailer from this value or capital in terms of the perception by customers of the quality of the goods and the prices of these goods at a certain time, namely merchandise value and differentiation value.

Merchandise value amounts to the customer's perception of the tangible and nontangible (i.e., quality) elements of a store's products weighed against the sacrifices (i.e., price, time, etc.) that the customer has to make to obtain these products. Differentiation value is the customer's perception of the favorable uniqueness of the store's quality relative to the quality of alternative stores. Whereas merchandise value occurs when good quality merchandise is offered for a low price (i.e., a "good deal"), differentiation value normally occurs when the highest quality (in terms of tangible and/or nontangible quality attributes) is offered at a higher price over that of other stores.

Note that merchandise value and differentiation value may be related to each other, that is, a store with merchandise value could also be associated with perceptions of uniqueness, perhaps based on the merchandise value or based on some other set of attributes (friendly personnel, store environment, etc.). Thus, there may be a number of reasons for a store to achieve differentiation value. For instance, in addition to the service and atmospheric elements of the store mentioned above, the store could also be symbolic of the consumer's aspirations and, thus, perhaps provide social reasons for setting the store apart in the consumer's mind. Overall, the concept of differentiation value is admittedly the result of many store-level influences, as is also true with the concept of merchandise value. I do not examine these influences here because these are at the level of stores (not the individual-level store outcomes that I am concerned with in this chapter) and because they have been examined in previous research (Baker, et al., 2002). I am more concerned in this chapter with the individual-level outcomes (perceptions, evaluations, intentions, and stated behavior) arising out of merchandise value and differentiation value. I acknowledge that there are many different sources of customer value (Sheth, Newman, & Gross, 1991), but I suggest that these all lead to the two main types of perceived value. Further, I limit this conceptualization to the customer value outcomes in a retail environment because this is where the retail literature is less revealing to date.

Inter- and Intraproduct Comparisons

Note that both types of value have "worth" and that, in both cases, shoppers feel that the price (low for merchandise value and high for differentiation value) is justified in terms of the quality obtained. The difference between the two constructs (although they may be related) accrues from the fact that they involve different comparisons by the consumer. This is in keeping with the notion of value in marketing and consumer research as involving some type of comparison (Holbrook, 1999). More specifically, the two types of value incorporate the two types of comparisons discussed by Oliver (1999). The first, an intraproduct comparison, is consistent with our definition of merchandise value, which involves a comparison of the benefits and costs within a single store. The second, an interproduct comparison, is consistent with differentiation value, which involves an assessment of the superiority of the store versus other stores. Keep in mind that, in both types of value, I am referring to a customer's overall perception of a store's value, not value perceived during a single store encounter.

Utilitarian versus Hedonic Outcomes

The rationale for suggesting only two basic types of value is grounded in the literature on marketing and consumer behavior, in which the notion of value has also been associated with two basic types—hedonic and utilitarian value (Babin, Darden, & Griffin, 1994; Batra & Ahtola 1991; Holbrook & Hirschman 1982). This is also in conformity with the definitions of merchandise value, which involves cognitions arising out of the consideration of the benefits versus costs (utilitarian value) of a store, and differentiation value, which leads to feelings of enjoyment and the like (hedonic value) arising out of the knowledge of the perceived superiority of certain attributes of a store versus other stores. For instance, Babin, Darden, and Griffin cite results obtained in focus groups in which consumers expressed delight in finding a store that was different from other stores.

However, I do not equate merchandise value and differentiation value with utilitarian and hedonic value, respectively. I suggest that utilitarian and hedonic value, as conceived by Babin, Darden, and Griffin (1994) and others refer to evaluative outcomes of the two types of customer value. I conceive of the two types of customer value as consumer perceptions about a store that lead to evaluative responses. In other words, merchandise value and differentiation value lead to utilitarian and hedonic value, respectively. In fact, consistent with this, Batra and Ahtola (1991) describe hedonic and utilitarian components of attitudes, which are evaluative in nature. The model in this chapter (see Figure 9.1) clearly differentiates among perceptions, evaluations, intentions, and behavioral outcomes. Because store perceptions are equivalent to beliefs, this is in conformity with accepted theoretical frameworks in psychology and consumer behavior (Assael, 1998; Fishbein & Ajzen, 1975). In sum, hedonic and utilitarian values are outcomes of customer value and not customer value itself.

Relatedly, note that merchandise and differentiation value are also different from consumer needs and consumer involvement. Consumer needs, or "felt deprivations" (Kotler & Armstrong, 2004), may be viewed as overarching consumer goals that are fulfilled during the shopping experience. As such, consumer needs will affect customer values and value outcomes, but they are not the same as perceptions of store value. The model in Figure 9.1 could be expanded to include consumer needs as an exogenous variable affecting perceptions of customer value. Similarly, we could include the level of a particular shopper's involvement with shopping as an exogenous variable that may well affect perceptions of value.

THE INFLUENCE OF CUSTOMER VALUE

In consonance with the concepts of hedonic and utilitarian value in the literature cited earlier, I suggest here that consumers derive a sense of pleasure in knowing that they have found a unique (in a desirable way) store that they can, and do, frequent. This suggestion is predicated on the notion of value as a function of both worth (Oliver, 1999) and scarcity. One fundamental tenet in the field of economics has been that value is increased when something of worth is in short supply (Samuelson, 1983). In general, I propose that consumers "like" (i.e., derive affect from) being in a store that is different in a good way. As mentioned earlier, previous research with focus groups (Babin, Darden, & Griffin, 1994) bears this out as well. Hence, I posit that affect explains (or mediates) why unique associations have usually been associated with loyalty and commitment (Assael, 1998).

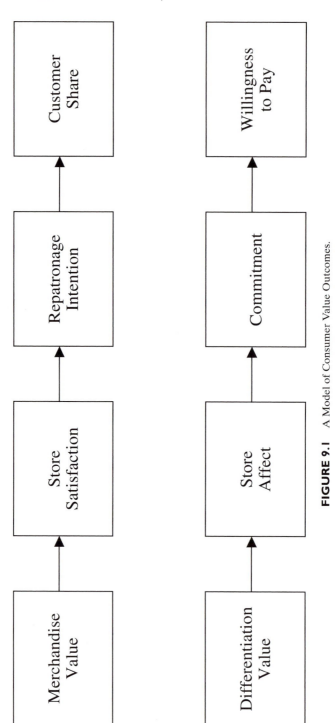

FIGURE 9.1   A Model of Consumer Value Outcomes.

Thus, I propose that people feel good when they find something of worth that is not abundantly available. This "feel good" feeling, as a result of breaking away from the ordinary and the mundane, is different from satisfaction in that it involves qualitative affects such as enjoyment and happiness. In contrast, satisfaction is an evaluative judgment (Oliver, 1997) and more cognitive in nature (Howard & Sheth 1969). Oliver also reviews evidence that satisfaction is a low arousal state, whereas qualitative affects are higher in arousal. Thus, satisfaction and positive affect, although they may be related to each other, are also sufficiently different from each other to allow us to propose that they have different antecedents and consequences.

Value versus Loyalty

Holbrook (1999) associates value with the situation and the consumer. Consistent with Woodruff and Gardial (1996), value is a function of individual needs and wants in a particular setting. This should be contrasted with the concept of loyalty, which is often associated with greater value (Sirdeshmukh, Singh, & Sabol, 2002) but is also usually suggested to be indifferent to situational demands (Oliver, 1999). Unlike value, loyalty is considered to be unaffected by the situation. Thus, value and loyalty are related but they are different constructs. In the model described next, I propose that they are related in two different ways via two different evaluative responses and that they result finally in two different behavioral outcomes.

Figure 9.1 depicts a hypothesized model of customer value outcomes in a retail environment. The model proposes that a customer perceives value in shopping at a particular store and forms an evaluation of his or her experience based on the realization of that value. The customer then forms an intention for future relations with the store and behaves in a corresponding manner. The model incorporates two specific routes to explain this response. The first route accounts for the functional, utilitarian component of decision making. If the customer perceives the store's offering to have merchandise value (e.g., "It is worth what I paid for it"), he or she will be satisfied and will likely return to the same store on future outings. As a result, that particular store will receive a greater share of its customers' purchases than its competitors. The second route focuses on the hedonic component of decision making. The customer perceives a store to have value because it is different from other stores. For reasons discussed in the previous section, this uniqueness arouses positive customer feelings, which in turn creates customer commitment to the store. Because of this high level of commitment, the customer is willing to pay a higher price at this store over other similar stores.

As an example, consider two very different stores. One is a high volume food store with a mass market appeal and a large variety of commonly used products and a large assortment of "value-priced" brands in each product category. Shoppers at this store avidly use the coupons and other sales promotions that the store offers each week. Shoppers leave the store satisfied with their purchases in terms of the deals and bargains that they were able to procure and they intend to return to take advantage of these promotions again. This store accounts for a high percentage of the total amount of the customers' weekly purchases. However, there is no special bond or connection with this store other than that the store offers plenty of bargains on a weekly basis. In other words, the basic appeal of the store is in its quality-price merchandise value.

In contrast, consider shoppers at a much smaller, low volume, high-priced food store that occupies a unique niche by providing a few products and a small assortment of high quality brands in each product category. Shoppers at this store do not expect sales and discounts from the store and the store does not offer these on a regular basis. Shoppers leave this store excited at having picked up a particularly fancy cake or a gourmet item that cannot be easily found in other stores. They also feel a bond or connection with this store that is not based on price and, in fact, they are well aware that they often pay a higher price for certain items at this store over other stores. However, in the minds of these shoppers, these prices are justified in terms of the unique atmosphere or the unique selection or quality of the products available at this store. These shoppers may not buy most of their food purchases for the week from this store, but they visit the store to buy a few expensive items that are not available elsewhere.

Let us now turn to explaining each of the constructs contained in the model in Figure 9.1 and formulating propositions for how these constructs link to each other.

CUSTOMER VALUE: MERCHANDISE VALUE AND DIFFERENTIATION VALUE

The definition of merchandise value in the previous section is consistent with the definition in the retail literature, where it has been defined as pertaining to the financial and other costs undertaken by the customer in order to obtain a product of appropriate quality. This element of customer value addresses the give-up versus get-back orientation of value. The customer perceives merchandise value when he or she obtains a product with specific attributes that enable him or her to accomplish some day-to-day task. The customer is likely to make the trade-off or sacrifice in terms of cost, because the offering performs in a certain way or because it has specific characteristics (i.e., it has utility). In the context of retail stores, the customer is likely to pick one store over another because that particular store stocks products/brands with certain attributes that are required by the customer, at a level of sacrifice that is considered to be appropriate for the utilitarian function achieved as a result.

Contrary to merchandise value, differentiation value (see the definition in the previous section) focuses on the uniqueness of the store and of its offerings. For example, perhaps the product/brand offerings are not mundane or ordinary, and the customer values this distinction from other alternatives.

Differentiation value influences the customer's more personal, "playful" side of decision making. The more novel product/brand offerings are meaningful because they tie into personal thoughts, feelings, and possibly experiences (Fournier, 1998; Holbrook & Hirschman, 1982; Ligas, 2000). Thus, the consumer shops at a specific retail establishment because some aspect of the experience is unique, whether it is the novel offerings, the stimulating atmosphere, or a combination of these and other unique traits. This fulfills a hedonic function in the consumer's life because this aspect is the pleasurable side of the shopping experience.

CUSTOMER RESPONSES: SATISFACTION AND POSITIVE AFFECT

Satisfaction can be defined as a cognitive evaluation resulting from the fulfillment of expectations. According to Howard and Sheth (1969), satisfaction is a cognitive state in which the buyer evaluates whether he or she has been adequately rewarded for the sacrifice he or she has undergone in obtaining the product. Thus, satisfaction is a "judgment," based on either a cognitive or emotional appraisal, made by the customer concerning whether his or her expectations were met (Oliver, 1997). It may well be a "judgment of one's emotions" (hence satisfaction and positive affect are correlated in the model), but it is not the actual feeling resulting from the experience (Barlow & Maul, 2000). When the customer evaluates whether a store's attributes are worth what he or she pays, he or she is likely making a judgment of the store's ability to meet his or her expectations, both in terms of quality and in terms of the sacrifice needed to obtain this quality. Thus, because expectations lead to satisfaction and merchandise value is the equivalent of a fulfillment of certain expectations, I argue that merchandise value will lead to satisfaction.

Positive affect is a pleasurable emotional response. When the customer experiences positive affect, he or she is likely to experience a number of specific emotions such as happiness, joy, or love (Bagozzi, Gopinath, & Nyer, 1999). Although these authors suggest that it is difficult to either easily categorize satisfaction as an emotion or to consider satisfaction as an appropriate "summary emotion," they do state that ". . . depending on the situation, product, and person—other positive and negative emotions are more important outcomes of purchase . . . [and] might be more valid reactions consumers have to purchases" (p. 201). Thus, the customer realizes a number of positive emotions as a result of the shopping encounter. Although the customer evaluates the experience satisfactorily, this evaluation does not completely summarize the experience. "If organizations want to consider total customer experiences, satisfaction by itself is a weak measurement . . ." (Barlow & Maul, 2000, p. 112).

As discussed and defined in the previous section, differentiation value is a positive and favorable perception of the unique nature of a store and, consequently, it positively affects the customer's affective evaluation of the shopping experience. In keeping with this, it has also been found that perceptions of differences are strongly associated with pleasurable feelings in a variety of product categories (Chaudhuri 1993). In sum, the uniqueness (in a good way) afforded by the store creates a positive experience for the customer (Babin, Darden, & Griffin, 1994), that is, an experience laden with positive emotional reactions (Holbrook & Hirschman, 1982). As a result, when a customer experiences greater differentiation value in the store, he or she will be more likely to feel greater positive affective responses toward the store.

CUSTOMER LOYALTY: REPATRONAGE AND COMMITMENT

Two aspects of loyalty, repurchase and attitudinal, have been well established in the marketing literature (Aaker, 1991; Chaudhuri & Holbrook, 2001; Dick & Basu, 1994; Jacoby & Chestnut, 1978; Oliver, 1999; Tucker, 1964). The repeat purchase side of loyalty is represented in our model as repatronage intentions, and the attitudinal side of loyalty is represented as commitment. The former type of loyalty pertains to a stated intent to rebuy from a particular store at a future date, whereas the latter refers to a positive attitudinal disposition toward a store based on a particular bond or connection with the store. Although the two aspects of loyalty are expected to relate to each other, they are also expected to have unique variances associated with different types of antecedents and consequences.

Prior research shows that satisfied customers are likely to be repeat purchasers, if for no other reason than that it is less effort to go with a "sure thing" than to switch to an unknown (Keaveney, 1995; Oliver, 1997). Thus, the customer is willing to purchase the offering again because, during prior consumption, the customer deemed the product/brand to be of a good quality (Zeithaml, 1988; Zeithaml, Berry, & Parasuraman, 1996). Although some prior research identifies a direct link between merchandise value and store patronage intentions (Baker, Parasuraman, Grewal, & Voss, 2002), other research indicates that satisfaction mediates the effect of quality on loyalty (Oliver). Thus, when considering all three constructs together, it is proposed that the customer receives a quality product for a fair price (high merchandise value), is satisfied with the consumption experience, and as a result returns to consume again. This leads to the proposition that as satisfaction increases, customers will be more likely to increase their repurchase intentions for a store.

The literature in retailing and consumer behavior has identified commitment as one's "motivation" to sustain a relationship with the other party, in our case the retailer (Bendapudi & Berry, 1997; Fournier, 1998). At the same time, the literature on emotion in interpersonal relationships strongly associates affect with any kind of relationship (Bersheid, 1983). Thus, because commitment (or attitudinal loyalty) is a relational intention, I propose here that positive affect will be positively related to commitment. Previous research also supports this for brands (Chaudhuri & Holbrook, 2001). Further, Barlow and Maul (2000, p. 113) state:

> Emotional accounts in commerce have to do with a reservoir of strong, positive feelings that are deposited and literally stored in customers' memory banks. Each strong positive emotional experience (both material and personal) helps connect the customer to the organization. . . .

Accordingly, a positive affective state motivates the customer to maintain the existing connection, that is to be committed to that store.

STORE OUTCOMES: CUSTOMER SHARE AND WILLINGNESS TO PAY

Willingness to pay is the propensity of a customer to pay a higher price at a particular store, even if another store offers the same or a similar item at a lower price. I define customer share (often referred to as "share-of-wallet") as the percentage of a customer's total monthly expenditure on a particular store type (say, bookstores) that is spent on a particular store (say, Barnes & Noble). Rust, Ziethaml, and Lemon (2000) emphasize the role of share-of-wallet in relational exchanges, in terms of profitability and customer lifetime value. Sirdeshmukh, Singh, and Sabol (2002) also state that share-of-wallet is one of the behaviors associated with relationship maintenance, thus I consider customer share to be an outcome of loyalty and, specifically, of repatronage intent.

Customer share is predicated on the double jeopardy effect (Ehrenberg, Goodhardt, & Barwise 1990), which propounds that loyal customers buy more of a certain brand. Prior research has also shown that repurchase intent is positively related to market share for brands but not to relative price, whereas attitudinal loyalty (commitment) is related to relative price but not to market share (Chaudhuri & Holbrook, 2001). Because customer share may be construed as the individual-level equivalent to market share for brands and willingness to pay as the equivalent of relative price, it is proposed that repurchase intent will lead to customer share but not to willingness to pay. On the other hand, commitment will lead to willingness to pay but not to customer share. Thus, it is suggested that customers can be committed to a particular store and pay high prices for a few items while also conducting most of their shopping elsewhere in less expensive stores. Therefore, greater repeat patronage will lead to greater customer share and greater customer commitment will lead to a greater willingness to pay.

The intent in the hypothesized model presented in Figure 9.1 has been to explain two distinct routes that represent customer value outcomes in a retail setting. A retail establishment is able to manipulate the consumption experience in a number of ways, such as by introducing/phasing out particular products/brands or by re-pricing (e.g., discounting, marking up) current offerings. In a more dramatic fashion, the retailer might alter its physical store environment. A model that attempts to identify and understand customer responses to such value-added acts needs to account for the effects of these various manipulations of the store experience. Therefore, the proposed model begins by identifying both merchandise and differentiation value. Merchandise value accounts for the value that the customer derives from the store based on its more functional or utilitarian manipulations (e.g., offering a lower price). Differentiation value deals with the value that the customer derives from the store's more hedonic undertakings (e.g., creating visually appealing store environments, merchandising offerings that other similar stores do not sell). Each value is evaluated differently by the customer, and each leads to a different relational intention. Ultimately, different store outcomes are realized as a result of these different customer values. In conclusion, a holistic perspective of customer value responses and their outcomes accounts for a more comprehensive understanding of the effects of retail strategies.

RESEARCH RESULTS

A Study of Value in Retailing

Purpose of the Study

To test the model in Figure 9.1.

Method

A consumer survey was conducted at a large retail store in a suburban area of North America. The store specializes in the sale of dairy, vegetables, fish, meat, and bakery products and also has sections for prepared food. Some national and regional food brands are sold at the store, but the bulk of the sales come from store brands in the various food categories. The store has weekly specials on sale and in general offers good merchandise value to its shoppers in terms of quality foods at affordable prices. In addition to food, the store has an annex for home and garden supplies. The store is well known in its region as a unique store specializing in quality dairy and food products with the added advantage of providing family entertainment during the shopping process. Examples of the store's entertainment appeal abound—a petting zoo on the premises, singing milk cartons, mooing ceramic cows, and so on. In addition to merchandise value, it was important to the study that the store provided an entertaining environment capable of arousing differentiation value and positive affect.

Consumers were asked to complete a self-administered survey after they had completed their shopping and were leaving the store. A total of 150 completed surveys were obtained. The survey respondents were largely female, working in white collar and professional careers, married with children, having an average household annual income above $100,000. These shoppers travelled anywhere from half a mile to 150 miles to come to the store. This indicates a certain level of commitment to the store, at least among some of the shoppers. Corstjens and Lal (2000) have shown that quality store brands can create store loyalty.

Results

Path analysis (using LISREL 8.52) was used to test the model and paths shown in Figure 9.2. In this path analysis, the multiple indicators were summed together for each construct, and the resulting summated score was used to represent that construct in the analysis. All of the paths in the proposed model were statistically significant (p > .05). However, examination of the modification indices showed that the model fit could be improved considerably by adding the paths from differentiation value to satisfaction and from store affect to repatronage intention. Accordingly, another path analysis was conducted in which these paths were included. This resulted in the following fit statistics: $\chi2(17) = 39.01$, P = .002, RMR = .04, GFI = .95, CFI = .98, IFI = .98. Standardized path coefficients for the model appear in Figure 9.2, which shows the results for all the significant paths in the final model at p < .05 or better. As diagrammed in Figure 9.2, the results indicate that merchandise value and differentiation value are indirectly related to store commitment and repatronage intent with the indirect linkages occurring through the constructs of store satisfaction and store affect. Of specific interest to the study as well is the relationship between store commitment and the purely endogenous variable, willingness to pay. Interestingly, in terms of the other purely exogenous variables in the study, although prior experience was directly related to commitment, affect, and repatronage intent, convenience was not. However, they were both positively related to each other.

The results vindicate the role of store satisfaction and store affect as mediating constructs in the relationship of value to commitment, and

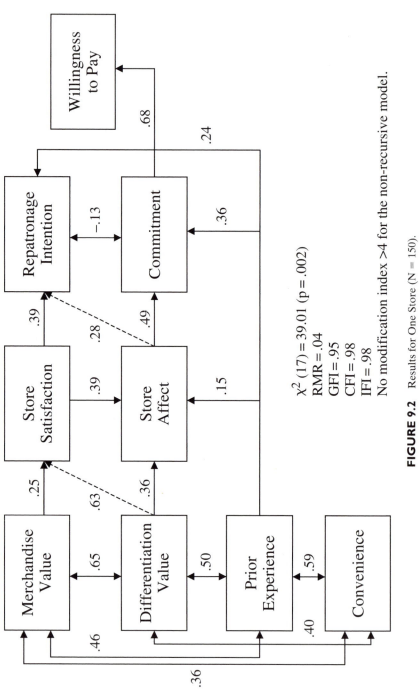

$\chi^2 (17) = 39.01 \ (p = .002)$
RMR = .04
GFI = .95
CFI = .98
IFI = .98
No modification index >4 for the non-recursive model.

FIGURE 9.2   Results for One Store (N = 150).

they should both continue to be examined in future studies of retail store relationships because they are shown here to be the link between store outcomes and the individual-level perceptions of value by store consumers.

In general, then, I find two clear pathways to store outcomes—one that is guided by reason and another that is routed through affect. The latter begins with prior experience and differentiation value and translates into either store satisfaction or store affect. Store affect and satisfaction, in turn, lead to store repatronge intentions. However, only store affect leads to store commitment, which directly influences shoppers' willingness to pay a higher price at a particular store.

Implications

Store managers can use these results to justify expenditures on promotions, which create long-term effects (such as store satisfaction and store affect) on consumers because it was found in this study that these constructs are related to store commitment and repatronage intention. This study vindicates the use of entertaining strategies to create positive store affect because such affect is demonstrated to lead to store commitment and, thus, to willingness to pay. The role of in-store entertainment appears from this study to be a viable strategy for creating greater store commitment. The use of music, animals, and other "delightful" diversions appears to lead people to like the store more and this, in turn, leads to commitment to the store.

This is in keeping with previous research by Hui, Dube, and Chebat (1997) who found that music created positive feelings and behavior towards a service provider. Kelley and Hoffman (1997) also found that positive affect was positively related to positive perceptions toward the service. However, both store affect and store satisfaction are needed for the store outcomes of commitment and repatronage. Consumers' satisfaction with a store can be increased by helpful and courteous service by store employees, consistent and fair prices, appropriate guarantees, and store return policies.

Further, this study helps to improve our overall understanding of the antecedents of store commitment, leading to improved marketing mix strategies. For instance, store communication strategies may be derived with special regard to the individual-level determinants of store commitment. One such implication for advertising, for instance, may be to demonstrate that all stores are not the same, to show the negative consequences of choosing the "wrong" store, and also to show the emotional consequences of choosing the "right" store by depicting positive store affect arising from the advertised store.

REFERENCES

Aaker, David A. (1991). *Managing brand equity: Capitalizing on the value of a brand name.* New York: Free Press.

Aaker, David A. (1996). Measuring brand equity across products and markets. *California Management Review, 38*(2), 102–120.

Adaval, Rashmi. (2001). Sometimes it just feels right: The differential weighting of affect-consistent and affect-inconsistent product information. *Journal of Consumer Research, 28,* 1–17.

Allport, G. W. (1935). Attitudes. In C. Murchison (Ed.), *A handbook of social psychology* (pp. 798–844). Worcester, Massachusetts: Clark University Press.

Alsop, Ronald. (1988, March 3). In TV viewers favorite 1987 ads, offbeat characters were the stars. *Wall Street Journal,* p. B1.

Amaldoss, Wilfred, & Jain, Sanjay. (2005). Pricing of conspicuous goods: A competitive analysis of social effects. *Joy Marketing Research, 92,* 30–42.

Anand, Punam, Holbrook, Morris B., & Stephens, Debra. (1988). The formation of affective judgements: The cognitive-affective model versus the independence hypothesis. *Journal of Consumer Research, 15,* 386–391.

Assael, Henry. (1998). *Consumer behavior and marketing action.* Cincinnati, OH: South-Western.

Averill, J. R. (1980). *A constructivist view of emotion.* In R. Plutchik and H. Kellerman (Eds.), Emotion: Theory, Research, and Experience. (pp. 305–339). New York: Academic Press.

Babin, Barry J., Darden, William R., & Griffin, Mitch. (1994). Work and/or fun: Measuring hedonic and utilitarian shopping value. *Journal of Consumer Research, 20,* 644–656.

Bagozzi, Richard P., Gopinath, Mahesh, & Nyer, Prashanth U. (1999). The role of emotions in marketing. *Journal of the Academy of Marketing Science, 27*(2), 184–206.

Baker, Julie, Parasuraman, A., Grewal, Dhruv, & Voss, Glenn B. (2002). The influence of multiple store environment cues on perceived merchandise value and patronage intentions. *Journal of Marketing, 66*(2), 120–141.

Baldinger, Allan L. (1990). Defining and applying the brand equity concept: Why the researcher should care. *Journal of Advertising Research, 30,* RC2–RC5.

Barlow, Janelle, & Maul, Dianna, (2000). *Emotional value: Creating strong bonds with your customers.* San Francisco, CA: Berrett-Koehler.

Barlow, Todd, & Wogalter, Michael S. (1993). Alcoholic beverage warnings in magazine and television advertisements. *Journal of Consumer Research, 20,* 147–156.

Barrett, Amy. (2003, June 9). Hot growth companies. *BusinessWeek,* 74–77.

Batra, Rajeev. (1986). Affective advertising: Role, processes, and measurement. In Robert A. Peterson, Wayne D. Hoyer, and William R. Wilson (Eds.), *The role of affect in consumer behavior* (pp. 53–86). Lexington, MA: Lexington Books.

Batra, Rajeev, & Ahtola, Olli T. (1991). Measuring the hedonic and utilitatian sources of consumer attitudes. *Marketing Letters, 2,* 159–170.

Batra, Rajeev, & Ray, Michael L. (1986). Affective responses mediating acceptance of advertising. *Journal of Consumer Research, 13,* 234–249.

Bauer, Raymond A. (1960). Consumer behavior as risk taking. In Robert S. Hancock (Ed.), *Dynamic marketing for a changing world* (pp. 389–398). Chicago, IL: American Marketing Association.

Bearden, William O., & Etzel, Michael J. (1982). Reference group influence of product and brand purchase decisions. *Journal of Consumer Research, 9*, 183–194.

Beatty, Sharon E., & Kahle, Lynn R. (1988). Alternative hierarchies of the attitude-behavior relationship: The impact of brand commitment and habit. *Journal of the Academy of Marketing Science, 16*(2), 1–10.

Belk, Russell W. (1988). Possessions and the extended self. *Journal of Consumer Research, 15*, 139–152.

Bello, D. C., & Holbrook, Morris B. (1995). Does an absence of brand equity generalize across product classes? *Journal of Business Research, 34*, 125–131.

Bendapudi, Neeli, & Berry, Leonard L. (1997). Customers' motivations for maintaining relationships with service providers. *Journal of Retailing, 73*(1), 15–37.

Berlyne, D. E. (1960). *Conflict, arousal, and curiosity.* New York: McGraw Hill.

Berscheid, Ellen. (1983). Emotion. In Harold H. Kelly (Ed.), *Close relationships* (pp. 110–168). New York: W. H. Freeman.

Bettman, James R. (1973). Perceived risk and its components: A model and empirical test. *Journal of Marketing Research, 10*, 184–190.

Bettman, James R. (1979). *An information processing theory of consumer choice.* Reading, MA: Addison-Wesley.

Bitner, Mary Jo. (1992). Servicescapes: The impact of physical surroundings on customers and employees. *Journal of Marketing, 56*, 57–71.

Blumenthal, Karen. (1995, May 26). Home buyers flock to fixed-rate mortgages. *Wall Street Journal,* C1.

Bolton, Ruth N. (1998). A dynamic model of the duration of the customer's relationship with a continuous service provider: The role of satisfaction. *Marketing Science, 17*(1), 45–65.

Bowen, Lawrence, & Chaffee, Steven H. (1974). Product involvement and pertinent advertising appeals. *Journalism Quarterly, 51*, 613–621.

Brendl, C. Miguel, Markman, Arthur B., & Messner, Claude. (2003). The devaluation effect: Activating a need devalues unrelated objects. *Journal of Consumer Research, 29*, 463–473.

Brown, Steven P., & Stayman, Douglas M. (1992). Antecedents and consequences of attitude toward the ad: A meta-analysis. *Journal of Consumer Research, 19*, 34–51.

Buck, Ross. (1976). *Human motivation and emotion.* New York: John Wiley.

Buck, Ross. (1984). *The communication of emotion.* New York: Guildford Press.

Buck, Ross. (1985). Prime theory: An integrated view of motivation and emotion. *Psychological Review, 92*(3), 389–413.

Buck, Ross. (1988). *Human motivation and emotion.* New York: John Wiley.

Buck, Ross. (1989). Emotional education and mass media. In R. P. Hawkins, J. M. Wiemann, & S. Pingree (Eds.), *Advancing communication science: Merging mass and interpersonal perspectives* (pp. 44–76). Beverly Hills, CA: Sage.

Buck, Ross. (1999). The biological affects: A typology. *Psychological Review, 106*(2), 301–336.

Buck, Ross, Anderson, Erica, Chaudhuri, Arjun, & Ray, Ipshita. (2004). Emotion and reason in persuasion: Applying the ARI model and the CASC scale. *Journal of Business Research, 57*(6), 647–656.

Buck, Ross, & Chaudhuri, Arjun, (1994). Affect, reason and involvement in persuasion: The ARI model. In P. Weinberg (Ed.), *Konsumentenforschung* (pp. 107–117). Munich: Vahlen.

Buck, Ross, Chaudhuri, Arjun, Georgson, Mats, & Kowta, Srinivas. (1995). Conceptualizing and operationalizing affect, reason and involvement in persuasion: The ARI model and the CASC scale. In F. Kardes & M. Sujan (Eds.), *Advances in consumer research* (Vol. 22, pp. 440–447). Provo, UT: Association for Consumer Research.

Burns, J. F. (1996, September 22). Denial and taboo blinding India to the horror of its AIDS scourge. *New York Times*, 1.

Burton, Scot, & Lichtenstein, Donald R. (1988). The effect of ad claims and ad context on attitude toward the advertisement. *Journal of Advertising, 17*(1), 3–11.

Cannon, W. B. (1927). The James-Lange theory of emotion: A critical examination and an alternative theory. *American Journal of Psychology, 39*, 106–124.

Chaiken, Shelly. (1980). Heuristic versus systematic information processing and the use of source versus message cues in persuasion. *Journal of Personality and Social Psychology, 39*(5), 752–766.

Chaiken, Shelly, & Eagly, Alice H. (1983). Communicator modelity as a determinant of persuasion: The role of communicator salience. *Journal of Personality and Social Psychology, 45*(2), 241–256.

Chaudhuri, Arjun. (1992). A theoretical framework for advertising. In Robert P. Leone & V. Kumar (Eds.), *Enhancing knowledge development in marketing, 1992 AMA educators' proceedings* (Vol. 3, pp. 442–446). Chicago: American Marketing Association.

Chaudhuri, Arjun. (1993). Advertising implications of the pleasure principle in the classifications of products. In W. Fred van Raaij & Gary J. Bamossy (Eds.), *European advances in consumer research* (Vol. 1, pp. 154–159). Provo, UT: Association for Consumer Research.

Chaudhuri, Arjun. (1996). The effect of media, product and message factors on ad persuasiveness: The role of affect and cognition. *Journal of Marketing Communications, 2*(4), 201–218.

Chaudhuri, Arjun. (2001). A study of emotion and reason in products and services. *Journal of Consumer Behavior, 1*(3), 267–279.

Chaudhuri, Arjun. (2004). Testing the independence of affect using prosocial and reptilian feelings. In William L. Cron & George S. Low (Eds.), *Marketing theory and applications* (Vol. 15, pp. 286–292). Chicago: American Marketing Association.

Chaudhuri, Arjun. (2005). Where's the affect? An investigation of the effect of three advertising scales on attitude to the AD. In Kathleen Seiders & Glenn B. Voss (Eds.), *Marketing theory and applications* (Vol. 16, pp. 161–167). Chicago: American Marketing Association.

Chaudhuri, Arjun, & Buck, Ross. (1990). Media differences in emotional responses to advertising. Unpublished study, University of Connecticut.

Chaudhuri, Arjun, & Buck, Ross. (1992). Advertising variables that predict consumer responses. In Robert P. Leone & V. Kumar (Eds.), *Enhancing knowledge development in marketing, 1992 AMA educators' proceedings* (Vol. 3, pp. 19–25). Chicago: American Marketing Association.

Chaudhuri, Arjun, & Buck, Ross. (1995). Media differences in rational and emotional responses to advertising. *Journal of Broadcasting & Electronic Media, 39*(1), 109–125.

Chaudhuri, Arjun, & Buck, Ross. (1997). Communication, cognition and involvement: A theoretical framework for advertising. *Journal of Marketing Communications, 3*(2), 113–125.

Chaudhuri, Arjun, & Holbrook, Morris B. (2001). The chain of effects from brand trust and brand affect to brand performance: The role of brand loyalty. *Journal of Marketing, 65*, 81–93.

Chaudhuri, Arjun, & Ray, Ipshita. (2003). Relationships between satisfaction, trust, and commitment in a retail environment. In Geraldine R. Henderson & Marian Chapman Moore (Eds.), *Marketing theory and applications* (Vol. 14, pp. 138–144). Chicago: American Marketing Association.

Chaudhuri, Arjun, & Ray, Ipshita. (2004). The effect of AIDS awareness on condom use intention among truck drivers in India: The role of beliefs, feelings and perceived vulnerability. *Journal of Marketing Communications, 10*(1), 17–34.

Chaudhuri, Arjun, & Watt, James H. (1995). An exploratory study of emotional attributes in radio commercials. *Journal of Marketing Communications, 1*(2), 61–70.

Cooley, C. H. (1902). *Human nature and the social order.* New York: Charles Scribner's Sons.

Corstjens, M., & Lal, R. (2000). Building store loyalty through store brands. *Journal of Marketing Research, 37,* 281–291.

Coulson, John S. (1989). An investigation of mood commercials. In Patricia Cafferata & Alice M. Tybout (Eds.), *Cognitive and affective responses to advertising* (pp. 21–30). Lexington, MA: Lexington Books.

Cox, Dena S., & Cox, Anthony D. (1988). What does familiarity breed? Complexity as a moderator of repetition effects in advertisement evaluation. *Journal of Consumer Research, 15,* 111–116.

Crispell, Diane. (1993, November 26). Negative feelings afflict 40 million adults in the U.S. *Wall Street Journal,* B1.

Cunningham, S. M. (1967). Perceived risk and brand loyalty. In D. Cox (Ed.), *Risk taking and informational handling in consumer behavior* (pp. 507–523). Boston, MA: Harvard University Press.

Daniels, Cora. (2003, June 9). J.C. Penney dresses up. *Fortune,* 127–130.

Darwin, Charles. (1872). *The expression of the emotions in man and animals.* London: John Murray.

Day, George S., & Wensley, Robin. (1988). Assessing advantage: A framework for diagnosing competitive strategy. *Journal of Marketing, 52,* 1–20.

deRivera, J. (1984). The structure of emotional relationships. In P. Shaver (Ed.), *Review of personality and social psychology* (Vol. 5, pp. 116–145), Beverly Hills, CA: Sage.

Dick, Alan S., & Basu, Kunal. (1994). Customer loyalty: Toward an integrated conceptual framework. *Journal of the Academy of Marketing Science, 22*(2), 99–113.

Doney, Patricia M., & Cannon, Joseph P. (1997). An examination of the nature of trust in buyer-seller relationships. *Journal of Marketing, 61*(2), 35–51.

Donthu, Naveen. (1994). Double jeopardy in television program choice. *Journal of the Academy of Marketing Science, 22*(2), 180–185.

Dowling, Grahame R., & Staelin, Richard. (1994). A model of perceived risk and intended risk-handling activity. *Journal of Consumer Research, 21,* 119–134.

Edell, Julie A., & Burke, Marian C. (1987). The power of feelings in understanding advertising effects. *Journal of Consumer Research, 14,* 421–433.

Ehrenberg, Andrew S. C., Goodhardt, Gerald J, & Barwise, T. Patrick. (1990). Double jeopardy revisited. *Journal of Marketing, 54*(3), 82–91.

Ekman, Paul, & Friesen, Wallace V. (1975). *Unmasking the face.* Englewood Cliffs, NJ: Prentice Hall.

Fader, P. S., & Schmittlein, D. C. (1993). Excess behavioral loyalty for high-share brands: Deviations from the Dirichlet model for repeat purchasing. *Journal of Marketing Research, 30,* 478–493.

Fishbein, M., & Ajzen, I. (1975). *Belief, attitude, intention, and behavior: An introduction to theory and research.* Reading, MA: Addison-Wesley.

Fitzgerald, Kate. (1994, January 10). Gizmos turn home protection into a boom. *Advertising Age,* S1.

Forest, Stephanie Anderson. (2003, June 2). Giving away the store. *BusinessWeek,* 51.

Fournier, Susan. (1998). Consumers and their brands: Developing relationship theory in consumer research. *Journal of Consumer Research, 24,* 343–373.

Freud, Sigmund. (1920). Beyond the Pleasure Principle. In Peter Gay (Ed.), *The Freud reader* (pp. 594–605). New York: Norton.

Freud, Sigmund. (1961). The ego and the id. In J. Strachey (Ed.), *The standard edition of the complete psychological works of Sigmund Freud* (pp. 19–27). London: Hogarth Press.

Gale, Bradley T. (1994). *Managing customer value: Creating quality and service that customers can see.* New York: The Free Press.

Garvey, Michael. (1994, May 23). Safer shopping. *Advertising Age*, 3.

Gerbner, George, & Gross, Larry. (1976, Spring). Living with television: The violence profile. *Journal of Communication*, 173–194.

Goffman, E. (1959). *The presentation of self in everyday life*. Garden City, NY: Doubleday Anchor.

Gorn, Gerald J. (1982). The effect of music in advertising on choice behavior: A classical conditioning approach. *Journal of Marketing, 46*, 94–101.

Gundlach, Gregory T., Achrol, Ravi S., & Mentzer, John T. (1995). The structure of commitment in exchange. *Journal of Marketing, 59*(1), 78–92.

Haley, Russell I., Richardson, Jack, & Baldwin, Beth M. (1984). The effects of nonverbal communication in television advertising. *Journal of Advertising, 24*(4), 11–18.

Hamouda, O. F. (1993). *John R. Hicks: The economist's economist*. Cambridge, MA: Blackwell.

Hansen, F. (1981). Hemispheric lateralization: Implications for understanding consumer behavior. *Journal of Consumer Research, 8*, 23–36.

Havlena, William J., & Holbrook, Morris M. (1986). The varieties of consumption experience: Comparing two typologies of emotion in consumer behavior. *Journal of Consumer Research, 13*, 394–404.

Heath, Timothy B. (1990). The logic of mere exposure: A reinterpretation of Anand, Holbrook and Stephens (1988). *Journal of Consumer Research, 17*, 237–244.

Hicks, John R. (1939). *Value and capital*. Oxford: Clarendon.

Hicks, John R. (1973). *Capital and time: A new-Austrian theory*. Oxford: Clarendon.

Higgins, T. E. (1987). Self-discrepancy: A theory relating self and affect. *Psychological Review, 94*, 319–340.

Holbrook, Morris B. (1999). *Consumer value: A framework for analysis and research*. New York: Routledge.

Holbrook, Morris B., & Batra, Rajeev. (1987). Assessing the role of emotions as mediators of consumer responses to advertising. *Journal of Consumer Research, 14*, 404–420.

Holbrook, Morris B., & Hirschman, Elizabeth C. (1982). The experiential aspects of consumption: Consumer fantasies, feelings, and fun. *Journal of Consumer Research, 9*, 132–140.

Holmes, Stanley. (2003, June 9). For Starbucks, there's no place like home. *BusinessWeek*, 48.

Howard, John A., & Sheth, Jagdish N. (1969). *The theory of buyer behavior*. New York: John Wiley.

Hui, Michael K., & Bateson, John E. G. (1991). Perceived control and the effects of crowding and consumer choice on the service experience. *Journal of Consumer Research, 18*, 174–184.

Hui, Michael K., Dube, L., & Chebat, J-C. (1997). The impact of music on consumers' reactions to waiting for services. *Journal of Retailing, 73*(1), 87–104.

Hunt Shelby, D., & Morgan, Robert M. (1995). The comparative advantage theory of competition. *Journal of Marketing, 59*, 1–15.

Jacoby, Jacob, & Chestnut, Robert. (1978). *Brand loyalty measurement and management*. New York: John Wiley.

Jacoby, Jacob, & Hoyer, Wayne D. (1990). The miscomprehension of mass media advertising claims. *Journal of Advertising Research, 30*(3), 9–16.

Jacoby, Jacob, & Kaplan, Leon B. (1972). The components of perceived risk. In M. Venkatesan (Ed.), *Proceedings of the third annual conference of the Association for Consumer Research* (pp. 382–393). College Park: MD: Association for Consumer Research.

James, William. (1890). *The principles of psychology* (Vol. 1). New York: Henry Holt.

Janis, I. L., & Field, P. B. (1959). Sex differences and personality factors related to persuasibility. In C. I. Hovland & I. L. Janis (Eds.), *Personality and Persuasibility* (pp. 55–68). New Haven, CT: Yale University Press.

Janiszewski, Chris. (1988). Preconscious processing effects: The independence of attitude formation and conscious thought. *Journal of Consumer Research, 15*, 199–209.

Jones, E. E. & Pittman, T. S. (1982). Toward a general theory of strategic self presentation. In J. Suls (Ed.), *Psychological perspectives on the self* (pp. 231–262). Hillsdale, NJ: Erlbaum.

Kanner, Bearnice. (1994, October 10). Americans feel in control. *Advertising Age, 52*.

Kardes, Frank. (1988). Spontaneous inference processes in advertising: The effect of conclusion omission and involvement in persuasion. *Journal of Consumer Research, 15*, 225–233.

Katz, Elihu J., Blumler, G., & Gurevitch, Michael. (1973). Uses of mass communication by the individual. *Public Opinion Quarterly, 37*, 504–516.

Keaveney, Susan M. (1995). Customer switching behavior in service industries: An exploratory study. *Journal of Marketing, 59*, 71–82.

Keller, Kevin L. (1993). Conceptualizing, measuring, and managing customer based brand equity. *Journal of Marketing, 57*(1), 1–22.

Kelley, S. W., & Hoffman, D. K. (1997). An investigation of positive affect, prosocial behaviors and service quality. *Journal of Retailing, 73*(1), 87–104.

Kelly, H. H. (1984). Affect in interpersonal relations. In P. Shaver (Ed.), *Review of personality and social psychology* (Vol. 5, pp. 89–115). Beverly Hills, CA: Sage.

Klapper, Joseph T. (1960). *The effects of mass communications.* Glencoe, IL: The Free Press.

Kohler, W. (1938). *The place of value in a world of facts.* New York: Liveright.

Kotler, Philip, & Armstrong, Gary. (2004). *Principles of marketing* (10th ed.). Upper Saddle River, NJ: Pearson Education.

Krugman, Herbert E. (1965). The impact of television advertising: Learning without involvement. *Public Opinion Quarterly, 29*, 349–356.

Krugman, Herbert E. (1971). Brain wave measures of media involvement. *Journal of Advertising Research, 11*(1), 3–9.

Krugman, Herbert E. (1977). Memory without recall, exposure without perception. *Journal of Advertising Research, 17*(4), 7–12.

Laurent, Gilles, & Kapferer, Jean-Noel. (1985). Measuring consumer involvement profiles. *Journal of Marketing Research, 22*, 41–53.

Lavidge, Robert J, & Steiner, Gary A. (1961). A model for predictive measurements of advertising effectiveness. *Journal of Marketing, 25*(3), 59–62.

Lazarus, Richard S. (1984). On the primacy of cognition. *American Psychologist, 39*, 124–129.

LeDoux, J. (1996). *The emotional brain: The mysterious underpinnings of emotional life.* New York: Simon and Schuster.

Lee, Louis. (2003, May 26). Thinking small at the mall. *BusinessWeek*, 94–95.

Leuthesser, L. (1988). *Defining, measuring, and managing brand equity: A conference summary.* Cambridge, MA: Marketing Science Institute.

Ligas, Mark. (2000). People, products, and pursuits: Exploring the relationship between consumer goals and product meanings. *Psychology and Marketing, 17*(11), 983–1003.

Lutz, Richard J., & Reilly, Patrick J. (1974). An exploration of the effects of perceived social and performance risk on consumer information acquisition. In Scott Ward and Peter Wright (Eds.), *Advances in consumer research* (Vol. 1, pp. 393–405). Chicago, IL: Association for Consumer Research.

MacInnis, Deborah J., & Stayman, Douglas M. (1993). Focal and emotional integration: Constructs, measures, and preliminary evidence. *Journal of Advertising, 22*, 51–66.

MacKenzie, Scott, & Lutz, Richard J. (1989). An empirical examination of the structural antecedents of attitude toward the ad in an advertising pretesting context. *Journal of Marketing, 53*, 48–65.

MacLean, Paul D. (1973). *A triune concept of the brain and behavior.* Toronto: University of Toronto Press.

MacLean, Paul D. (1990). *The triune brain in evolution.* New York: Plenum Press.

MacLean, Paul D. (1993). Cerebral evolution of emotion. In M. Lewis & J. Haviland (Eds.), *Handbook of emotions* (pp. 67–83). New York: Guilford Press.

Mandler, George. (1975). *Mind and emotion.* New York: John Wiley.

Mandler, George. (1982). The structure of value: Accounting for taste. In Margaret Sydnor Clark and Susan T. Fiske (Eds.), *Cognition and affect* (pp. 3–36). Hillsdale, NJ: Lawrence Erlbaum.

McCarthy, M. J. (1991, March 22). Mind probe. *Wall Street Journal*, p. B3.

McEwen, William J, & Clark Leavitt. (1976). A way to describe TV commercials. *Journal of Advertising Research, 16*(6), 35–39.

McLuhan, Marshall H. (1964). *Understanding media: The extension of man.* New York: McGraw Hill.

McPhee, William N. (1963). *Formal theories of mass behavior.* New York: Free Press.

McQuarrie, Edward F., & Munson, Michael J. (1987). The Zaichkowsky personal involvement inventory: Modification and extension. In Melanie Wallendorf and Paul Anderson (Eds.), *Advances in consumer research* (Vol. 14, pp. 36–40). Provo, UT: Association for Consumer Research.

Mead, George H. (1934). *Mind, self, and society.* Chicago: University of Chicago Press.

Mehrabian, Albert, & Russell, James A. (1974). *An approach to environmental psychology.* Cambridge, MA: MIT Press.

Mitchell, Andrew, & Olson, Jerry C. (1981). Are product attribute beliefs the only mediator of advertising effects on brand attitude? *Journal of Marketing Research, 18*, 318–332.

Moorman, Christine, Zaltman, Gerald, & Deshpande, Rohit. (1992). Relationships between providers and users of market research: The dynamics of trust within and between organizations. *Journal of Marketing Research, 29*, 314–328.

Moreland, R. L., & Zajonc, Robert B. (1977). Is stimulus recognition a necessary condition for the occurrence of exposure effects? *Journal of Personality and Social Psychology, 35*, 19–199.

Morgan, Robert M., & Hunt, Shelby D. (1994). The commitment-trust theory of relationship marketing. *Journal of Marketing, 58*(3), 20–38.

Muehling, Darrel D., & McCann, Michelle. (1993). Attitude toward the ad: A review. *Journal of Current Issues and Research in Advertising, 15*(2), 25–58.

Murphy, Patrick E., & Enis, Ben E. (1986). Classifying products strategically. *Journal of Marketing Research, 50*, 24–42.

Okada, Erica M. (2005). Justification effects on consumer choice of hedonic and utilitarian goods. *Journal of Marketing Research, 92*, 43–53.

Oliver, Richard L. (1997). *Satisfaction: A behavioral perspective on the consumer.* Boston, MA: Irwin McGraw-Hill.

Oliver, Richard L. (1999). Whence consumer loyalty? *Journal of Marketing, 63*, 33–44.

Olney, Thomas J., Holbrook, Morris B., & Batra, Rajeev. (1991). Consumer responses to advertising: The effects of ad content, emotions, and attitude toward the ad on viewing time. *Journal of Consumer Research, 17*, 440–453.

Park, C. S., & Srinivasan, V. (1994). A survey-based method for measuring and understanding brand equity and its extendibility. *Journal of Marketing Research, 31*, 271–288.

Park, C. Whan, & Young, S. Mark. (1986). Consumer response to television commercials: The impact of involvement and background music on brand attitude formation. *Journal of Market Research, 23*, 17–24.

Parks, Jerry. (1995, June 12). Road worriers. *Advertising Age*, 3.

Pavlov, I. (1927). *Conditioned reflexes. An investigation of the physiological activity of the cerebral cortex.* London: Oxford University Press.

Pechmann, Cornelia, & Stewart, David A. (1989). The multidimensionality of persuasive communications: Theoretical and empirical foundations. In Patricia Cafferata and Alice M. Tybout (Eds.), *Cognitive and affective responses to advertising* (pp. 31–45). Lexington, MA: Lexington Books.

Perry, Ralph B. (1926). *General theory of value: Its meaning and basic principles construed in terms of interest.* Cambridge, MA: Harvard University Press.

Perugini, Marco, & Bagozzi, Richard P. (2001). The role of desires and anticipated emotions in goal-directed behaviours: Broadening and deepening the theory of planned behavior. *British Journal of Social Psychology, 40,* 79–98.

Pessemier, E. A. (1959). A new way to determine buying decisions. *Journal of Marketing, 24,* 41–46.

Petty, Richard E., & Cacioppo, John T. (1986). *Communication and persuasion: Central and peripheral routes to attitude change.* New York: Springer-Verlag.

Pham, Michael T., Cohen, Joel B., Pracejus, John W., & Hughes, G. David. (2001). Affect monitoring and the primacy of feelings in judgment. *Journal of Consumer Research, 28,* 167–188.

Plutchik, R. (1980). *Emotion: A psychoevolutionary synthesis.* New York: Harper and Row.

Pollay, Richard W. (1986). The distorted mirror: Reflections on the unintended consequences of advertising. *Journal of Marketing, 50,* 18–35.

Porter, Michael E. (1980). *Competitive Strategy.* New York: The Free Press.

Preston, I. L. (1970). A reinterpretation of the meaning of involvement in Krugman's models of advertising communication. *Journalism Quarterly, 47,* 287–295.

Ratchford, Brian T. (1987, August/September). New insights about the FCB grid. *Journal of Advertising Research,* 24–38.

Ray, Michael L. (1973). Marketing communication and the hierarchy of effects. In P. Clarke (Ed.), *New models for mass communication research.* Beverly Hills, CA: Sage.

Ray, Michael L., & Batra, Rajeev. (1983). Emotion and persuasion in advertising. *Advances in Consumer Research, 10,* 543–548.

Reichheld, Frederic F. (1996). *The loyalty effect: The hidden force behind growth, profits and lasting value.* Boston: Harvard Business School Press.

Rickard, Leah. (1994, November 7). Spirituality, hope on horizon as solace sought. *Advertising Age,* S1, S14.

Robertson, Thomas S. (1976). Low-commitment consumer behavior. *Journal of Advertising Research, 16,* 19–24.

Rogers, C. (1951). *Client centered therapy.* Boston: Houghton Mifflin.

Rogers, Everett M. (1983). *Diffusion of Innovations.* New York: Free Press.

Roseman, I. J. (1984). Cognitive determinants of emotion. In P. Shaver (Ed.), *Review of personality and social psychology* (Vol. 5, pp. 11–36). Beverly Hills, CA: Sage.

Rosenberg, Milton J. (1956). Cognitive structure and attitudinal affect. *Journal of Abnormal and Social Psychology, 53,* 367–372.

Rossiter, John R., Percy, Larry, & Donovan, Robert J. (1991). A better advertising planning grid. *Journal of Advertising Research, 31*(5), 11–21.

Russell, Bertrand. (1912). *Problems of philosophy.* New York: Oxford University Press.

Rust, Roland T., Zeithaml, Valarie A. & Lemon, Katherine N. (2000). *Driving customer equity: How customer lifetime value is reshaping corporate strategy.* New York: The Free Press.

Samuelson, Paul A. (1983). *Foundations of economic analysis.* Cambridge, MA: Harvard University Press.

Schacter, Stanley, & Singer, Jerome E. (1962). The cognitive, social, and physiological determinants of emotional state. *Psychological Review, 69,* 379–399.

Scheff, T. J. (1984). The taboo on coarse emotions. In P. Shaver (Ed.), *Review of personality and social psychology* (Vol. 5, pp. 146–169). Beverly Hills, CA: Sage.

Sewall, Murphy, & Sarel, Dan. (1986). Characteristics of radio commercials and their recall effectiveness. *Journal of Marketing, 50*(1), 52–60.

Shaver, Phillip, Schwartz, Judith, Kirson, Donald, & O'Connor, Cary. (1987). Emotion knowledge: Further exploration of a prototype approach. *Journal of Personality and Social Psychology, 52,* 1061–1086.

Shelley, Percy B. (1993). Shelley. Poems. New York, NY: Random House.

Sheth, Jagdish N., Newman, Bruce I., & Gross, Barbara L. (1991). *Consumption values and market choices: Theory and applications.* Cincinnati, OH: South-Western.

Sheth, Jagdish N., & Parvatiyar, Atun. (1995). Relationship marketing in consumer markets: Antecedents and consequences. *Journal of the Academy of Marketing Science, 23*(4), 255–271.

Silverstein, Michael J., & Fiske, Neil. (2003). *Trading up.* New York: Portfolio.

Simmons, Jacqueline. (1995, June 2). Car rental insurance? Heed unposted warnings. *Wall Street Journal,* p. B1.

Sirdeshmukh, Deepak, Singh, Jagdip, & Sabol, Barry. (2002). Consumer trust, value, and loyalty in relational exchanges. *Journal of Marketing, 66*(1), 15–37.

Smith, Daniel C., & Park, C. Whan. (1992). The effects of brand extensions on market share and advertising efficiency. *Journal of Marketing Research, 29,* 296–313.

Srinivasan, Narasimhan, & Ratchford, Brian T. (1991). An empirical test of a model of external search for automobiles. *Journal of Consumer Research, 18,* 233–242.

Statistical Policy Division (1987). *Standard Industrial Classification Manual.* Washington, D.C: Government Printing Office.

Stayman, Douglas M., & Aaker, David A. (1988). Are all the effects of ad-induced feelings mediated by AAD? *Journal of Consumer Research, 15,* 368–373.

Stewart, David W., & Furse, David H. (1986). *Effective television advertising: A study of 1000 commercials.* Lexington, MA: Lexington Books.

Stewart, David W., & Koslow, Scott. (1989). Executional factors and advertising effectiveness: A replication. *Journal of Advertising, 18*(3), 21–32.

Swann, William B., Jr. (1983). Self-verification: Bringing social reality into harmony with the self. In J. Suls & A. G. Greenwald (Eds.), *Social psychological perspectives on the self* (Vol. 2, pp. 33–66). Hillsdale, NJ: Erlbaum.

Swann, William B., Griffin, John J., Predmore, Steven C., & Gaines, Bebe. (1987). The cognitive-affective crossfire: When self-consistency confronts self-enhancement. *Journal of Personality and Social Psychology, 52*(5), 881–889.

Thomas, Emory. (1995, June 15). An Olympic feat: Keeping terrorists away. *Wall Street Journal,* p. B1.

Tomkins, Silvan S. (1962). *Affect imagery consciousness* (Vol. 1). New York: Springer.

Traylor, Mark B. (1981). Product involvement and brand commitment. *Journal of Advertising Research, 26*(6), 51–56.

Tsal, Yehoshua. (1985). On the relationship between cognitive and affective processes: A critique of Zajonc and Markus. *Journal of Consumer Research, 12,* 358–362.

Tucker, D. M. (1981). Lateral brain function, emotion, and conceptualization. *Psychological Bulletin, 89,* 19–46.

Tucker, W. T. (1964). The development of brand loyalty. *Journal of Marketing Research, 1,* 32–35.

Upshaw, L. B. (1995). *Building brand identity.* New York: John Wiley.

Van Trijp, Hans C. M., Hoyer, Wayne D., & Inman, J. Jeffrey. (1996). Why switch? Product-category level explanations for true variety-seeking behavior. *Journal of Marketing Research, 33,* 281–292.

Vaughn, Richard. (1980). How advertising works: A planning model. *Journal of Advertising Research, 20*(5), 27–33.

Vaughn, Richard. (1986, February/March). How advertising works: A planning model revisited. *Journal of Advertising Research,* 57–66.

Voss, Kevin E., Spangenberg, Eric R., & Grohmann, Bianca, (2003). Measuring the hedonic and utilitarian dimensions of consumer attitude. *Journal of Marketing Research, 40,* 310–320.

Watson, J. B., & Rayner, R. (1920). Conditioned emotional responses. *Journal of Experimental Psychology, 3,* 1–14.

Webster, M., & Sobieszek, B. (1974). *Sources of self evaluation.* New York: John Wiley.

Weinstein, Sidney, Appel, Valentine, & Weinstein, Curt. (1980). Brain activity responses to magazine and television advertising. *Journal of Advertising Research, 20*(3), 57–63.

Willeford, W. (1987). *Feeling, imagination, and the self.* Evanston, IL: Northwestern University Press.

Winters, Lewis C. (1991). Brand equity measures: Some recent advances. *Marketing Research, 3,* 70–73.

Woodruff, Robert B., & Gardial, Sarah F. (1996). *Know your customer: New approaches to understanding customer value and satisfaction.* Malden, MA: Blackwell.

Wright, Peter L. (1974). Analyzing media effects on advertising responses. *Public Opinion Quarterly, 38,* 195–205.

Wylie, Ruth C. (1968). The present status of self theory. In E. F. Borgatta and W. W. Lambert (Eds.), *Handbook of personality and research* (pp. 728–787). Chicago: Rand McNally.

Yeung, Catherine W. M., & Wyer, Jr., Robert S., (2004). Affect, appraisal and consumer judgment. *Journal of Consumer Research, 31,* 412–424.

Zaichkowsky, Judith L. (1985). Measuring the involvement concept. *Journal of Consumer Research, 12,* 341–352.

Zaichkowsky, Judith L. (1986). Conceptualizing involvement. *Journal of Advertising, 15*(2), 4–14.

Zaichkowsky, Judith L. (1987). The personal involvement inventory: Reduction and application to advertising. Working paper, Simon Fraser University.

Zaichkowsky, Judith L. (1994). The personal involvement inventory: Reduction, revision, and application to advertising. *Journal of Advertising, 23*(4), 59–69.

Zajonc, Robert B. (1980). Feeling and thinking: Preferences need no inferences. *American Psychologist, 35,* 151–175.

Zajonc, Robert B., & Markus, Hazel. (1982). Affective and cognitive factors in preferences. *Journal of Consumer Research, 9,* 123–131.

Zeithaml, Valarie A. (1988). Consumer perceptions of price, quality, and value: A means-end model and synthesis of evidence. *Journal of Marketing, 52,* 2–22.

Zeithaml, Valarie A., Berry, Leonard L., & Parasuraman, A. (1996). The behavioral consequences of service quality. *Journal of Marketing, 60*(2), 31–46.

INDEX